S0-BTB-711

Education

*TO WHOM
DOES IT BELONG?*

Education

TO WHOM DOES IT BELONG?

BY
JOSEPH P. LOCIGNO

FOREWORD BY JAMES O'GARA

 DESCLÉE COMPANY INC.
New York - Tournai - Paris - Rome

97542

377.82
L 812

This edition first published in 1968 by Desclée Co., Inc., of New York.

Nihil obstat
Daniel V. FLYNN, J. C. D.
Censor librorum

Imprimatur
Terence J. COOKE, D. D.
Auxiliary Bishop of New York
New York, N. Y., December 23, 1967

All rights reserved

Library of Congress Catalog Card Number : 68-22237.

Printed in Belgium by Desclée & Cie, Éditeurs, S. A., Tournai

TABLE OF CONTENTS

FOREWORD

Parochial schools may not be divisive, but the school question is. Indeed, it is probably safe to say that no question in American life is more calculated to set Catholic Christian against Protestant Christian or Catholic against Jew, and this is odd. On the surface, at least, there are questions infinitely more divisive. Is Jesus the Savior? Is he the son of God? Did he establish a Church? Is this Church the new Israel? What was Peter's role, and what should be that of his modern-day successors? At first glance it would seem that such questions would be the controversial ones rather than the school question. But at second look we see it is really not so odd that the school issue should be so divisive, for the Catholic parochial school stands as a brick-and-mortar symbol of that Church's admittedly large claims. As so much in our history testifies, it is dreadfully easy for the Protestant or Jew confronting the question of federal aid to see, not American Catholic children, but the fearful Church of Rome.

This is not the place to rehearse the struggle over federal aid to parochial schools. It is, however, the correct place to express the hope that the principal subject of this book, shared time, be judged as much as possible apart from the ancient animosities that pervade so much of the discussion of the school issue. This may be a vain hope, for it is easier to open than to heal old wounds, but a calm consideration of the philosophy and background of shared time would be invaluable.

Shared time means exactly that—a sharing of the school time of children between the state-supported schools and religious schools. It grants that the state may require that the child attend school, but it emphasizes that the state does not and should not have total control. Shared time is one way of allowing Church and State to share the child's time at the discretion of the parent. Thus it represents, at least potentially, a radical shift from the present situation in which there are religious schools to which some children go exclusively and public schools to which other children go equally exclusively.

In this volume, Father Joseph Locigno gives some idea of how shared time would and in some places does work. Are there difficulties? There are, many. Are there situations in which shared time probably would not work at all? Again the answer is clearly yes. But are there places and educational situations in which shared time could work wonders? Once more the answer is yes, and the purpose of this book is to encourage a sober look at these possibilities.

Shared time recognizes that Americans differ in their religious beliefs. It recognizes the rights of the parent in education without denying the needs of the community as a whole. It stresses the fact that we in America need as much unity as we can get without sacrificing essential differences. All these are plus factors, but they are not all. As a Catholic I must face the fact that less than half of the Catholic children in the United States are in religious schools and that this percentage is declining. We know that the one-time goal of every Catholic child in a Catholic school is impossible, completely aside from the question of whether it is a goal we would now wish to pursue. How are we to provide for the needs of those children who do not now receive religious education in any coherent, organized fashion? Shared time is not the whole answer by any means, but under the right conditions it is one answer. The shared time idea testifies that religion does have a place in education; it affirms that society has a stake in passing on moral and religious values, even though Church and State are separate, and it allows us to do something about this affirmation.

Here it would be good to emphasize that Catholics should not be the only ones concerned with this problem—far from it. Protestants and Jews confront a problem in the field of religious education that may be even more pressing than that of Catholics. The plain fact is that millions of American children are growing up with little or no contact with their religious roots. This should be a matter of concern to us all.

How are we to avoid the spread of religious illiteracy? There is no one answer. Religious schools as they now exist are one way; released time is another. Teaching about religion in the public schools and shared time are two other methods which have not yet been sufficiently tried. I know that shared time comes under attack from two sides. On the one hand, some Catholic parents who are intent on receiving what they see as their just due in the shape of federal aid for parochial schools regard shared time as a dangerous side-issue. On the other hand, there are Protestant and Jewish groups which dismiss the whole shared time idea as just another Catholic raid on the federal treasury.

In my view, both of these reactions are mistaken. Shared time deserves to be judged on its own merits. It is not a Protestant-Jewish stalking-horse to divert attention or funds from the parochial school; it is not a Catholic stalking-horse to get the taxpayer's money into the hands of the hierarchy. It is instead a serious effort to provide one solution to a knotty problem that has bedeviled us for many years—not the total answer but one part of it. The difficulties involved are very real; at first glance the shared time idea looks like an impossibly ambitious attempt to reconcile hopelessly divergent goals and ambitions and viewpoints. Indeed, in the abstract it is hard to imagine that shared time can be made to work, but this means only that shared time is much like the American idea itself. To me shared time under certain circumstances seems like a pragmatic, particularly American answer to a peculiarly American problem. On that basis it is certainly worth serious consideration.

New York City   James O'Gara
Jan. 19, 1968

INTRODUCTION

In this critical era, the Catholic Church is undergoing a renewal and rethinking in all phases of its life. Under consideration is a reexamination of the teaching mission of the Church. Realizing that the goal of every Catholic child in a Catholic school is neither feasible nor possible, and that each year less and less of its children are being educated in its schools, many Catholic educators are investigating whether a total commitment to education is necessary for the Church to fulfill its ministry. It is with good reason then that almost half of the Catholic school systems in the United States are engaged in a cooperative effort with the public schools to educate children. Numerous grade schools and high schools are engaged in a form of educational activity called shared time education.

The main impetus to shared time education has come from Protestant quarters. Few Catholic educators have endorsed the concept of shared time. Leaders like Lawrence Cardinal Shehan of Baltimore; Bishop Stephen S. Woznicki of Saginaw, Michigan; Bishop John B. McDowell of Pittsburgh, and Bishop William W. McManus of Chicago have been enthusiastic. However, by and large most Catholic educators have been cautious. Yet the program should be of concern to all educators whether they are in Catholic or public schools, since shared time could have significant impact on educational policies in general and upon public and Catholic schools specifically.

However, a number of Catholic educators are still devoted to a concept of the Church's total commitment to education. If shared time is accepted, they would question whether the program has a legitimate place within the magisterial fabric of the Church.

This work is undertaken with the purpose of demonstrating that shared time education is in conformity with the role of the Church as educator and is therefore not contrary to the Church's mission to educate. In fact cooperation between Church and State is in the very best Catholic and American tradition with the Church and the State serving as cooperators in education under the direction of the parents.

The approach used to demonstrate the role of the Church and the State in shared time education will begin with a consideration of the theory of shared time. Various notions will be investigated; its basic rationale will be expressed, and finally, statements of leading advocates of the program will be presented.

Then there will be an investigation of the general principles governing, especially in this country, the relations between the Church and the State. The interpretation of the American experience is that of Gustave Weigel and John Courtney Murray. It will be shown that Church and State should cooperate for the spiritual and temporal good of their members who belong to both orders. Shared time education casts this cooperation into an existential form.

The historical presentation will consist of two fundamental considerations. The first is that shared time education is in conformity with the Jeffersonian concept of the role of the Church and the State in education. The second is that the Church assumed a total commitment to education in the United States because of conditions which no longer exist on the American scene. Various forms of cooperation between Church and State in education did appear from time to time, and if the ecumenical climate had been different, they might have been successful. The concepts of Thomas J. Bouquillon as expressed in his work, *Education: To Whom Does It Belong?*, although sharply criticized from 1891-1895, prophetically called for the harmonious cooperation of the child, the family, the Church and the State in education.

The agents of education, the parents, the Church and the State, and their proper roles to educate will be reexamined, especially in the light of Vatican II and the Declaration on Christian Education. Parents have the right to determine where and for how much and for how long each agency should be involved in the education of the child. The Church has the right to require that the child be instructed in the faith, but the State has the right to supervise the child's education for the total good of society.

From a pragmatic point of view it will be shown from case histories that shared time does work. One form or other of shared time actually has been in effect for the past forty years and has been successful.

Finally attention will be directed to problems which are related to shared time. These will be considered under the form of objections from Catholics, administrative problems, and lastly, the problem of legality.

The presentation will largely remain in the realm of the theoretical. However, it is hoped that the work will encourage the practical application of the concept.

For their encouragement and criticism at various stages of this work, I thank Professors Edward Power, Pierre Lambert, and Michael Anello, and Sister Josephina Concannon of Boston College. Evelyn Hartung, Sister Ellen Weaver, and Roger Rainville were most gracious in either typing the manuscript or commenting on the drafts of the chapters. Dom Jerome Hayden of Marsalin encouraged me always in my search for excellence.

Finally, a dedication here seems most appropriate. To Peter and Jessie Locigno, without whom this would have been an impossibility, we dedicate this work.

Why a total commitment?

By virtue of the words of Christ to the apostles, "Go, therefore, and make disciples of all nations, baptizing them in the name of the Father, and of the Son, and of the Holy Spirit, teaching them to observe all that I have commanded you," [1] "go into the whole world and preach the Gospel to every creature," [2] the Catholic Church possesses the office of teacher.

> That divine mission, entrusted by Christ to the apostles, will last until the end of the world, since the Gospel they are to teach is for all time the source of all life for the Church. And for this reason the apostles, appointed as rulers in this society, took care to appoint successors. [3]

Christ, then, set the Church on its course to teach and preach the good news, that is, the coming of the Kingdom, the new people of God, which for centuries had been promised in the Scriptures.

The Church of Christ which in the Creed is professed as one, holy, catholic, and apostolic is constituted and organized in the world as a society and is governed by the successor of Peter and by the

[1] Mt 28:19-20.

[2] Mk 16:15.

[3] Second Vatican Council, *Constitution on the Church* (Washington: National Catholic Welfare Conference, 1964), p. 21.

bishops in communion with him. The Pope and the college, or body of bishops, receive from Christ, to whom was given all power in heaven and on earth, the mission to teach all nations and to preach the Gospel to every creature, so that all men may attain to salvation by faith, baptism, and fulfillment of the commandments. To fulfill this mission Christ promised and sent the Holy Spirit to the apostles, by whose power they would be "witnesses to him before nations and peoples, and kings, even to the ends of the earth. . . . And that duty, which the Lord committed to the shepherds of his people, is a true service, which in sacred literature is significantly called *diakonia* or ministry." [4] For the Pope and the bishops are "authentic teachers, that is teachers endowed with the authority of Christ, who preach to the people committed to them the faith they must believe and put into practice. . . ." [5]

In its early years this then was the ministry of service which the Church engaged in, the teaching and preaching of the Word of God. The *diakonia* was to educate in faith and morals, and this took place during the sacred liturgy or in the homes of the faithful.

> In fact, during the first three centuries after Christ there was no such thing as a Christian school. There were schools that were attended by Christian boys and girls, schools in which Christians taught, and schools— if we may call them that—in which prospective Christians were prepared for entrance into the Church.

[4] *Ibid.*, p. 26.
[5] *Ibid.*, p. 27.

But none of these, individually or together, fulfilled the modern sense of the word school.

The early Church did not have schools of its own. One reason was that the Church did not want them, either because she did not think they were important or because she did not have the time or the energy to look after them. The Church regarded her mission as being on a level that was supraschool and may be even supra-educational. [6]

Christian schools with a formal, literary commitment were slow in coming. The Church was content to allow the faithful to attend the well-established system of classical schools already in operation. During the fourth century in the West the monastic schools began to accept a definite literary commitment. However, with the decline of the classical-Roman system of education the Church was compelled to establish schools or do without them. From then on the Church's *diakonia* to educate was no longer merely in the area of faith and morals, but in the establishment and maintenance of schools in every branch of learning from nurseries to universities. With the passing of time the Church assumed a total involvement in education.

When Catholics journeyed to the new world, they searched for a better social climate in which to live and work. At first, though few in number, Catholics generally supported the development of the common or public schools. However, the American Catholic child was not made to feel at

[6] Edward J. Power, *Main Currents in the History of Education* (New York: McGraw Hill, 1962), p. 152.

home in the public school.   After 1840, when efforts
to obtain public support for New York parochial
schools failed, Catholic interest and energy began to
be expended almost exclusively on the schools of
the Church, leaving the public schools as a semi-
Protestant domain.   During the immediate period
following the Civil War, universal education began
to take hold everywhere.   By 1880, public school
enrollment reached one million; by 1900, it had
soared to fifteen million and by 1920 to twenty-one
million.   Catholic school enrollment also began to
mount.   At the turn of the century, following the
impetus of the school legislation passed in 1884 by
the Third Plenary Council of Baltimore, there were
854,523 pupils in Catholic schools and by 1920, this
number had more than doubled to 1.8 million. [7]

An ideal of Catholic education posited by the
Third Council of Baltimore has been every Catholic
child in a Catholic school.   After eighty years of
almost superhuman exertion to realize this ideal, it
remains as distant as always.

> In elementary schools grades 1-8, for the school year
> 1962-63, according to the official infant baptisms reported
> with all attrition rates applied, the total eligible Catholic
> youth was 8,315,555.   The total reported enrollment was
> 4,342,273.   This enrollment represents 52.21 percent of
> those eligible elementary school youth.   On the same
> basis the number eligible for secondary school grades
> 9-12 was 3,131,574, and the reported enrollment was
> 1,009,081, or 32.22 percent of those eligible.   For a
> combined total for grades 1-12, we find the demograph-

[7] Daniel Callahan (ed.), *Federal Aid and Catholic Schools*
(Baltimore: Helicon, 1964), pp. 31-33.

ically processed infant baptism figure at 11,447,129 and
the total reported enrollment, grades 1-12, at 5,351,354
or 46.74 percent of those eligible in actual enrollment. [8]

The study of Catholic education sponsored by
the Carnegie Corporation with the cooperation of
the University of Notre Dame, which provided the
above figures, made a statistical projection of what
the 1968-69 school year might look like for Catholic
elementary and secondary schools. In the projection
the same baptism figures, the same percent of enrollment, the same staff-to-pupil ratios, the same room
and facility usage are brought ahead for seven years.

Over 9,777,108 children would be eligible for
elementary school enrollment. Using the 1962-63
percentage of 52.21, over 5,100,000 children would
be enrolled in these schools. This would mean an
increase of 748,700 elementary pupils without increasing or decreasing the percentage of pupils
served. An addition of 12,644 religious teachers and
6,322 lay teachers would be required. An additional
16,860 rooms would be needed at an estimated cost
of $ 227,610,000 (at $ 13,500 per room). [9]

On the secondary level, 4,154,080 students
would be eligible for enrollment in Catholic high
schools. Using the 1962-63 percentage of 32.22,
there would be 1,338,444 students actually enrolled.
This would mean an increase of 329,363 secondary
pupils to be served in 1968-69. An additional 8,445
religious teachers and 4,223 lay teachers would be

[8] Reginald A. Neuwien, (ed.), *Catholic Schools in Action*
(Notre Dame: University of Notre Dame Press, 1966), p. 33.
[9] *Ibid.*, p. 36.

required.   A conservatively estimated cost for needed building facilities would be $494,000,000 (at
$1,550 per student). [10]

In July of 1963, the Archdiocese of Cincinnati,
through the chairman of the school board, Auxiliary
Bishop Paul F. Leibold, announced that no further
school construction was to be undertaken until there
were sufficiently trained teachers and funds to com-
pensate them.   The Diocese of Rochester, New
York, announced that after September of 1963, for
the immediate future there would be a ban on new
schools and on the expansion of existing ones.   In
1962, Joseph Cardinal Ritter, the late Archbishop of
St. Louis, laid down a similar policy for his Archdiocese; and shortly before his death in 1967 the
Cardinal went so far as to question the real need
for Catholic schools.   The Bishops of Saginaw,
Spokane, Kansas City, Fargo, Richmond, and Green
Bay have all been forced to adjust to the shortage of
teachers and classrooms by curtailing one or more
of the grades in their schools.

The archbishops and bishops of the country
have no intention of abandoning Catholic education.
Demands by parents for Catholic schools have not
slackened.   Spot checks of diocesan school systems
show that Catholic schools have been forced to turn
away thousands of applicants for both the elementary
and secondary grades, and where enrollments have
been curtailed this has been due to a desire for
smaller classes and a search for excellence on the
part of school authorities.

[10] *Ibid.*

With the advent of Sister-formation programs and the attracting and holding of better and more qualified lay teachers, the quality of Catholic elementary and secondary schooling, like that of public schools, is steadily improving. Despite the impressive accomplishments of Catholic schools over the past eighty years, Catholic leadership is beginning to realize that many patterns of the past have served their purpose. New approaches, new emphases, and new methods are called for.

At the same time, the renewal, the rethinking, the rebirth, and reform which the Church is undergoing as a result of the efforts of Popes John XXIII and Paul VI and the effects of Vatican Council II have caused many to reexamine the teaching mission of the Church. Is a total commitment to education truly necessary for the Catholic Church to fulfill its ministry of service to the world? Does the mandate to teach given the Church by Christ demand the conducting of kindergartens, vocational and technical schools, and the teaching of electronics, the use of computers, and involvement in other scientific fields requiring costly equipment and highly trained teachers?

Whatever the answers may be to these questions, in no way would the right of the Chruch to a total role in education be denied. What is questioned however, from historical reality and the existential fact that less than fifty percent of Catholic children are in Catholic schools, is whether it would be wiser for the Church to search for ways and means whereby its commitment to education would be directed more toward the preaching and the teaching of the Word of God and those disciplines immediately associated with values, leaving neutral subjects to another agency, namely the State or public schools.

By analogy, during the nineteenth century, the Church was deeply involved in the political life of Europe through its control of the Papal States in Italy. At no time in history was the Church more a temporal and spiritual power and the Pope literally a king and a bishop. In 1871, under the command of Giuseppe Garibaldi the Papal States were seized and Pius IX became a voluntary prisoner in the Vatican. It was not until 1929, during the Pontificate of Pius XI that the Roman Question was settled by the Lateran Treaty, and the temporal sovereignty of the Pope over 108.7 acres within the city of Rome was recognized.

For many churchmen the loss of the Papal States and the consequent removal of the Church from the political arena were considered serious tragedies. Yet today, theologians and historians of the Church look upon the seizure of the Papal States as the start of a new era in the Church. No longer should the Church directly involve itself in the temporal and the political. Now the Chruch could truly dedicate itself to the saving of souls through pastoral activity. Given impetus by the events of 1871, the Church assumed a new hue. From then on the Church began to evolve into what Christ intended it to be, the people of God. The Church as a society could divest itself of temporal ways, means, forms, methods and honors. In no way would the right of the Church to rule in the temporal order be denied, but this role should be limited for the fulfillment of its ministry to service. Similarly, in regard to education, history and existential reality might well dictate that the Church should limit her commitment to teach.

The crisis facing American Catholic education has its counterpart in a major problem facing public schools in the country in regard to religious training. During the past hundred years, Americans have witnessed the gradual retreat in our public schools from a Protestant expression of religious training and worship, to a gradual elimination of any form of religious practice or teaching. In the 1960's, almost every type of religious practice has been challenged. Most parents recognize the desirability of religious education for their children, but they are aware of the difficulty of achieving this in the public schools.

This is the distressing situation which confronts public school administrators and teachers. They are fully aware of the importance of religion to the American way of life, but they are acutely conscious of the restrictions which hamper their efforts. Neutrality in religion has become part of the public school code. Such a position was intended to achieve a conservative, objective, and intelligent separation of Church and State without hampering the temporal interest of the one or the spiritual interest of the other. Unhappily, this position has resulted in a general secularization of children, society, and institutions. For the good of all children, whether they be Catholic or not, and whether they attend Catholic or public schools, an answer must be found so that their religious development will be secured.

Many solutions have been proposed and tested. Some have sought for a logical, systematic development of religious knowledge, on a gradual basis, and, most important, a program comparable with that available in content and approach with the so-called secular subjects. It was also hoped for that the inclusion of religious ideals, interpretations, and judgments would take place when and where they normally occurred in other disciplines. At one time it was thought that the answer would be the inclusion of religion, on a voluntary basis, taught by trained teachers of religion in the public schools. In the minds of the children religious education would be at least equivalent in importance to secular education. The latter approach was outlawed by the Supreme Court while the former approaches have failed.

Many have looked to the released time program for an answer. The Supreme Court has declared that religious education could be given during school time off public school property. Catholic and Protestant representatives agree that the program is not adequate and in fact difficult and cumbersome. The Jewish community generally opposes it. Overall, the program has experienced a high degree of failure.

The hours arranged for instruction are sometimes inconvenient. It is difficult to secure qualified teachers to conduct released time classes because many of them are already carrying heavy teaching schedules in parochial elementary or secondary schools. The children find it a great inconvenience and respond to it with varying degrees of disinterest. It is difficult to provide on a once-a-week basis anything that resembles a systematic program or to sustain interest when the gaps between classes are so lengthy.

The removal of opening exercises which included the recitation of prayers, Bible reading, and other religious exercises from public school classrooms may not of itself be of any serious loss to religious education. Prior to any decision by the Supreme Court, six State courts had already declared Bible reading unconstitutional. These States included Wisconsin, Illinois, Ohio, Louisiana, South Dakota, and Washington. The Supreme Court of Florida in 1962, enjoined religious observances of Christmas, Easter, and Hanukkah holidays in the public schools.

It is difficult to believe that any child learns much about God from the rote recital of prayer or from hearing a teacher or fellow student mumble through a few verses from the Psalms. However, these religious trimmings have had a symbolic meaning to many parents, especially Protestants. As long as prayers were recited each day at the start of school, parents were able to find comfort in the fact that the modest amount of religious instructions their children received at home and at Sunday school was being reinforced by the public school. The Supreme Court has destroyed this myth and has forced parents to take a realistic look at the religious education of their children. What they see is not very reassuring.

> Jewish children enrolled in synagogue schools receive about 200 hours of religious instruction annually. Catholic children (including those in public schools) get at least 100 hours of formal training in religion. But a Protestant child, even if he attends Sunday School faithfully, receives only about 25 hours of religious instruction a year. " All of the years that a child spends in Sunday school add up to about two months, " says the Rev. Dr. W. Kent Gilbert, a Philadelphia Lutheran educator. Dr. Carl F. H. Henry, editor of *Christianity Today*, agrees that " it is small wonder the average child in most Protestant homes can give no adequate reason for his faith. " [11]

What then can be done to procure for children the opportunity for religious instruction, for the development of spiritual and social values which are essential to the individual and society? Can religious educators cooperate with public school administrators in order to accomplish this necessary goal? Perhaps some educators are satisfied with released time programs. Many Catholics would like to maintain the status quo but efforts should be made to obtain funds from the State or Federal Government. However, the constitutionality of direct federal or State aid to grade and secondary schools has yet to be decided by the Supreme Court and even if direct aid were bestowed upon Catholic schools it would still

[11] Louis Cassels, " A Way Out of Our Parochial-Public School Conflict, " *Look*, XXVI (August 28, 1962), p. 59.

be questionable whether the Church could accomplish its aims, both individual and common, with the increased Catholic population. Although some Catholic educators have won "converts" to the cause of equal aid for all children, no matter what schools they attend, even in this age of ecumenical dialogue and understanding, many Protestants and Jews are still vehement about federal or State aid to children attending Catholic schools.

Something must be done and it seems no longer possible to accomplish our aims, whether in public or Catholic schools, by the use of means or forms which we have depended upon in the past. One dynamic concept has been brought to light by Robert F. Drinan, Dean of Boston College Law School.

Reflecting upon recent Supreme Court decisions divesting the public schools of the last two of its major pan-Protestant symbols, Bible reading and the recitation of prayers, Father Drinan believes that public school officials have been told in bluntest terms in June, 1963, by Justice Thomas C. Clark, writing for a majority, that "one's education is not complete without a study of comparative religion or the history of religion." Drinan notes that a commission of the American Association of School Administrators has recognized the need to find appropriate means to deal effectively with religion as one of the most important influences in man's history.

Recently aroused interest in religion on the part of public school officials may be due more importantly, however, to the undeniable fact that responsible critics have in recent years asserted that the omnipresent silence about religion in the public schools may be so thunderous that it is bringing about the establishment of a philosophy of education which is the equivalent of secular humanism. The public schools have both unconsciously and deliberately avoided dealing with the history and impact of religion although there was nothing unconstitutional about such study. Perhaps the lack of qualified teachers and the scarcity of usable materials have been used as an excuse.

A course in the history of religion could be given by a committed Christian or non-Christian in a scholarly and academic way. A scholarly, religious person could be qualified to give an objective course. Although care should be taken not to offend the values of non-believers, competent and courageous steps should be used to give the subject of religion an academic position in the curriculum comparable to the position given to every subject from art to zoology.

Although the suggestions of Dean Drinan are both dynamic and encouraging, in themselves courses in the history of religion and comparative religion would only be value drops in an academic bucket. Lest educators and administrators fall into the Socratic fallacy, it would be well to recall that knowledge does not necessarily of itself lead to virtue, nor does studying about religion lead to religious living.

From what has been written, it is then evident

why a new concept, shared time education, has appealed to many Catholic and Protestant educators, as well as to some Jewish leaders, as an answer to Church-State problems in education. There is some hope that the concept may provide a common ground for agreement.

In numerous school districts in the United States, non-public school pupils are attending public schools for instruction in one or more subjects during a regular school day. The practice, in itself, is not new. Arrangements involving relationships between American public and non-public schools have been made from time to time for the purpose of educating children and youth. However, only in recent years has it been called "shared time education" and received national attention. In view of President Johnson's education message to the 89th Congress on January 12, 1965, shared time has gained the attention of educators, church leaders, legislators, and the public in general.

In simplest terms the proposal consists of a sharing of the school time of children between State-supported schools, which provide general education in a denominationally neutral context, and Church-supported schools which proceed with a specific denominational religious emphasis. [12] The definition emphasizes sharing the child's time between the school directed by the Church and the school directed by the State. The assumption is that the time of the child until he reaches the age of

[12] Harry L. Sterns, *Shared Time—A Symposium* (New York: Religious Education Association, 1962), p. 5.

majority is under the direction of his parents who, although they must see to it that their child is educated, may make their own decisions as to what that education shall be and may choose the agency to provide it. Although the State may demand that the child attend school, it does not have full and complete control of the child. Shared time then aims to bring the State and the Church into a sharing of the education of the child at the discretion of the parents. It revises the notion that there are Church schools which claim all of the time of some children and public schools which claim all of the time of others.

Shared time then brings together as cooperators in the education of children public and non-public schools. A public school is a school operated by publicly elected or appointed school officials in which the program and activities are under the control of these officials and which is supported by public funds; while a school designated as non-public is established by an agency other than the State, subdivisions of the State, or the Federal Government, which usually is supported primarily by other than public funds, and the operation of whose program rests with other than publicly elected or appointed officials.

Since its use by Harry L. Stearns in 1961, the term shared time has taken on many meanings. Some educators prefer to use the term "dual enrollment" since shared time has often been confused with another form of publicly operated assistance to all children called shared services. One example of the latter is sending public school teachers into non-public schools for educational programs (e.g. remedial reading) in which the public has a special interest. No school is compelled to take the teachers, but neither does any private school have a choice or ultimate control over the teacher it gets. The teachers are chosen by the public school boards and are responsible to them. The programs in which the teachers assist the children are chosen by the Federal and State Governments.

Included in shared services would also be the use of library resources and printed and published instructional materials. Library sources would contain books, periodicals, documents, magnetic tapes, phonograph records, charts and textbooks. These library resources and instructional materials must be approved by an appropriate State or local educational authority for use, or are used in public elementary or secondary schools of the State. Religious texts are therefore excluded. Other services which are shared by children from both public and Catholic schools are counselling, testing programs, educational television, teaching machines, and taped lessons.

Throughout this study the term shared time will continue to be used because of its popularity and prevalent usage in the current literature. Other names suggested are split time, reserved time, educational cooperation, part-time enrollment, and dual registration.

The theory of
shared time education

In a survey conducted by the National Education Association it was discovered that thirty-five States have one or more school systems operating a shared time program. States reporting the largest number of school systems with such a program are: Michigan with 42; Ohio, 36; Pennsylvania, 31; Illinois, 27; Wisconsin, 25; Minnesota, 13; Indiana, 11; and Missouri, 10. [1] A 1967 study by the National Education Association further indicated that in those cases where there is shared time, primarily it is in the area of non-academic subjects (industrial arts, home economics, driver training, etc.). [2] The National Catholic Educational Association revealed that almost half of the dioceses are engaged in some form of shared time activity. In 55 dioceses there are over 250 grade schools and 180 high schools where at least a minimum of shared time is in operation. [3] With so

[1] Research Division—National Education Association, *Shared-Time Programs: An Exploratory Study*, Research Report 1964—R 10, 1964, p. 7.

[2] Research Division—National Education Association, *Public School Cooperation with Non-Public Schools* (not yet published).

[3] Terry Ferrer, " Catholic Education in Ferment, " *New York Herald Tribune* (April 25, 1965), p. 34.

many programs of shared time in effect and with the possibility that the program may be adopted by many more, it would be well to consider its underlying theory.

The term shared time has been defined by the United States Office of Education as

> ...an arrangement whereby a child or youth regularly and concurrently attends a public school part-time and a non-public school part-time, pursuing part of his elementary or secondary program of studies under the direction and control of the public school and the remaining part under the direction and control of the non-public school. [4]

Francis Keppel, former United States Commissioner of Education has defined shared time as "a dual enrollment of a child in a private (mostly Catholic schools in the United States) and a public school." [5] Bishop John P. McDowell, Superintendent of Schools of the Diocese of Pittsburgh, considers shared time in its simplest terms as "an arrangement whereby children attending parochial schools would be able to take certain courses in the parochial school and other courses in the public schools." [6] Shared time means simply that all students in a community would come together in the public school for

[4] Department of Health, Education, and Welfare—Office of Education, " Dual Enrollment—Cast Study " (Washington, 1964) (Mimeographed), p. 1.

[5] Gerald Grant, " Shared Time Test Urged by Keppel, " *Washington Post* (February 29, 1964), p. 6.

[6] John P. McDowell, " Shared Time, " *C.E.A.P. Bulletin*, XVI (Summer 1962), p. 11.

the religiously neutral courses while those who so desired could attend a parochial school for instruction in those subjects in which religion is an integral part. The common element of these definitions is that the time of the child is shared between the State supported schools and the religious or non-public schools.

An example of a shared time program could be the following: sixty children attend a public school from 8 : 30 a.m. to 11 : 30 a.m. on Mondays through Fridays during the school year to study mathematics, science, and art, and also attend a Catholic school from 11 : 45 a.m. to 3 : 00 p.m. on Mondays through Fridays during the same school year to study social studies, English, and religion. Or, as another example, forty children attend a public school from 1 : 30 p.m. to 3 : 15 p.m. each Wednesday during the school year to study woodwork and homemaking, and during the remainder of each school week attend the non-public school to pursue the balance of their program of studies.

Shared time has often been confused with the concepts of shared facilities and released time. Shared time is distinguished from shared facilities which are either: 1) public school buildings, sites, or equipment regularly used without rental fee by non-public schools pupils who are under the immediate supervision and control of non-public school officials, or 2) non-public school buildings, sites, or equipment regularly used without rental fee by public school pupils who are under the immediate supervision and control of public school officials. (For example,

100 pupils of a non-public school use the gymnasium of the neighboring public school each weekday from 2 : 30 p.m. to 3 : 30 p.m. for physical education classes and are taught by a teacher of the non-public school. Or, as another example, the pupils of a public school use the football field of a neighboring non-public school for all of their "home" inter-scholastic football games.)

The concept of shared time is quite different from the notion of released time education. Released time carries with it the implication that the State controls all of the schooling of the child in the public school, but may release some part of the time to various denominations for religious instructions. Shared time implies in a much stronger degree the basic principle, stated in the judicial dicta of the Oregon School Case, that the child is much more the child of the parent than of the State and that, under parental judgment, the time for formal education shall be apportioned to the school and/or the Church or other recognized agency on a basis of dividing or sharing the responsibility of the child's total education.

Shared time then is more than an extended released time program. Its philosophy is entirely different. Released time actually misrepresents the role of religion, the parent, and the State. It grants an hour a week to religious instruction by way of concession; it implies that the right of the State to educate comes first; it makes religion seem a mere appendage to the educational curriculum. Shared time, on the other hand, is meant to express pragmatically the joint interest of the Church and State in the educational process.

Underlying the theory of shared time is the basic moral concept that the child is the creature of his parents who have control over his life, his nurture, and his time until he reaches the age of majority and his own independence. The right is not absolute, since parents may not take the life of the child, and they must give him reasonable care and support.

The child, too, is the creature and creation of God who has instituted the family among men and has entrusted the child to the parents. The Church, likewise founded by God, has a stake in the education of the child. In a pluralistic tradition, the various churches (denominations) may fulfill their teaching role by merely providing a place where the parents may bring their children to worship or by providing actual schools which teach not only religion but secular subjects as well.

The State makes claim to the child as a future citizen. The totalitarian State claims all of the child's time and turns the child from both his God and his parents. The democratic State, on the other hand, seeks to produce free, educated citizens who are literate and think critically. In a truly democratic State there will not be one system of education, but many: public, parochial, and private, each contributing various hues of experience in the vast search for truth and knowledge. The State in a free society will uphold the primary right of parents and the right of the Church to educate, but at the same time the State will have the right to require that each child be educated as a free citizen. However, the State may never become the sole master of the child.

Basic to shared time is the recognition that Americans do differ in their religious beliefs. It recognizes the right of parents and the right of the Church to educate without ignoring the needs of the State. Parents must submit to State regulations that their children be educated, but they make their own decision what that education will be and may choose what agency will accomplish this.

A consideration will be given to a question: What subjects would be studied in each school and why? Perhaps it would be better to answer the why first.

For the Catholic school the division of subjects would have to be made on the basis of value content. Every school has a philosophy of education which states the immediate and ultimate aims of the school. Through directed experiences the school attempts to develop in the child the understandings, attitudes, opinions, values, and ideals in line with its philosophy of education. In both the public and Catholic schools there is a definite philosophy of education. All the experiences which the child has in the school and which are planned by the school are calculated to attain certain objectives. In terms of these ultimate philosophic values, everything is finally resolved or interpreted.

As the gamut of school disciplines is viewed it is apparent that certain subjects are more involved with values than others. In fact, certain subjects have as their immediate goal the development of such values. Some disciplines achieve this end only indirectly and remotely. Bishop McDowel divides the subjects in the program of studies into two broad groups:

> The first of these would include religion, guidance, social studies, fine arts, science and English. These subjects are directly concerned, in varying degrees, with value content and ideals and are, again in varying degrees, intended to achieve philosophical objectives immediately. Obviously religion is directly concerned with values. Science on the other hand, while concerned with values because of interpretations required and because of certain moral and spiritual guides which are inherent, would be concerned with values in a less direct way. There is a scale with these subjects which makes them more or less directly concerned with values. In the second group we may list those courses or programs which are less directly concerned with values. Under this heading I would list languages, mathematics, the practical arts, commercial subjects, safety, and physical education. [7]

From this it must not be assumed that McDowell excludes per se any subjects from the value field. Basic to Catholic education is the concept that its philosophy should permeate every discipline, even when the content is "neutral." Obviously there is a hierarchy of values and every subject in the curriculum is not related in the same way to the philosophical objectives in that such ends are or can be achieved with equal success in each course.

[7] McDowell, *op. cit.*, p. 11.

Many Catholic educators, especially those devoted to particular subjects, may disagree with McDowell's twofold division. To those who are critical of his views McDowell writes: "To such objections I would reply that it seems better to me to provide all the children with a fine education in the value subjects, than to offer a few a full program in all subjects, some of which are less directly related to philosophical objectives." [8]   However, this is an area of shared time which should be carefully studied by Catholic educators to discover precisely what value contents each subject contributes.

Shared time is not entirely a new concept. "A 1963 study prepared by the legislative reference service of the Library of Congress states that limited shared time programs have been in operation for forty years or more; actually Pittsburgh has known a shared time course in the practical arts since 1913." [9]   However, it has only been in recent years that the notion has moved beyond the theoretical or modified stages and into the realm of pure shared time, where the school hours of the student are divided (or shared) in time proportion and subject importance between the parochial and public schools of the student's enrollment.

Most, if not all, of the schools engaged in shared time are Catholic. Yet, it may be of surprise to know that the birth of shared time, or its introduction into the educational market place, is largely

[8] *Ibid.*

[9] John G. Deedy, " The Share Time Experiment, " *Commonweal*, LXXIX (January 13, 1964), p. 530.

due to a series of Protestant initiatives. Perhaps the first of these was the publication in 1956 by Dr. Erwin L. Shaver of the Council of Churches in Massachusetts of the work, *The Weekday School Church*. In this much discussed book Shaver outlines the advantages of the growing practice throughout the United States of having children whose primary enrollment is in a Catholic school, taking some of their courses in the public schools, [10] "even to the extent in one reported instance of a 50-50 program." [11]

In September 1961, Dr. Harry L. Stearns, the then Superintendent of Schools in Englewood, New Jersey, and a member of the Board of Christian Education of the United Presbyterian Church, United States of America, in an article in *Christianity and Crisis*, coined the very phrase shared time. [12] Stearns has pushed shared time through his writings and lectures.

On November 22, 1960, about forty Protestant and Catholic officials met privately at the Woodner Hotel in Washington, D. C., to discuss topics of common concern, including the question of religious exercises in public schools and the controversy over aid to parochial schools. Each side had restated its own views and no agreement seemed in sight.

[10] Erwin L. Shaver, *The Weekday School Church* (Boston: Pilgrim Press, 1956), p. 7.

[11] Edward Wakin, " The Shared Time Experiment—How it Operates, " *Saturday Review* (February 15, 1964), p. 68.

[12] Harry L. Stearns, " ' Shared Time ' Answer to an Impasse, " *Christianity and Crisis*, XXI (September 18, 1961), pp. 154-57.

Stearns then suggested shared time as a step in the right direction. [13]

Stearns' suggestion brought a spark of life to the meeting. It was decided to hold another private meeting, with Jewish leaders and public school officials attending. The second meeting was held at the Interchurch Center in New York on October 11, 1961. Some had doubts at the meeting about shared time, but the consensus of the gathering was expressed by Rabbi Arthur Gilbert of New York: " It is worth a try. "

One group (Protestant and Catholic) saw shared time increasing the religious literacy of America's children; a second (Jewish and Protestant) took a sociological view and envisioned shared time as a bridge over divisiveness; a third (Protestant, Catholic and Jewish) approached shared time as the answer to the federal aid to education impasse. Whatever the logic, balance, legitimacy or validity of the individual schools, it was the Catholics who put shared time to test, thus moving discussion from the conference rooms and the journals of opinion into the arena of actuality.

Another milestone in the history of shared time was the publication of the January-February 1962 issue of *Religious Education*. The thirty-page symposium consists of an exposition of the shared time proposal by Stearns, and nineteen commentaries by educators, mainly applauding his initiative but point-

[13] Gerald Grant, " Shared Time Might be Key to Church School Aid Puzzle, " *Washington Post* (February 17, 1963), p. E-2.

ing out possible weaknesses as well as possible advantages.

In November 1962, the Committee on Religion and Public Education and the Committee on Weekday Religious Education, both of the National Council of Churches of Christ in the United States, met in New York to discuss shared time. The National Council of Churches of Christ, meeting in St. Louis, Missouri, in February 1963, established a new department of Church and Public School Relations to study shared time possibilities.

The first formal interest on the part of the Federal Government came on May 6, 1963, when Adam Clayton Powell, chairman of the United States House of Representatives Committee on Education and Labor, introduced a bill on behalf of the Kennedy administration to amend the National Defense Education Act of 1958. The Bill, H.R. 6074, would have provided five million dollars for the fiscal year ending June 30, 1964, and a like sum for each of the two succeeding fiscal years for making payments to local agencies in education for the acquisition of equipment suitable for use in shared time programs in the areas of science, mathematics, or modern foreign languages; for the minor remodeling of laboratories or other space used for such equipment, and for the administration of such shared time programs. Although the bill itself did not reach a floor vote in the House of Representatives, the hearings before the Congressional subcommittee studying shared time, together with pertinent information, appeared in a book on shared time which many have considered the unofficial " bible " of the program. [14]

On March 18, 1964, an all day interfaith meeting, consisting of twenty-five religious and civic leaders was held at the Harvard Club in Boston. At the meeting Herold Hunt, who holds the Eliot Chair of Education at Harvard University, told the group that shared time programs may well be the answer to America's problems centering on religious education. " Practically, " Hunt said, " the problem is to intelligently and constitutionally relate the secularism or neutrality of the public school, which is essential in a pluralistic society, and the religious imperative on the part of many persons that the experiences in the curriculum be in some way related to religion. " [15] At the meeting, Dr. Gerald E. Knoff of the National Council of Churches, aired the problems facing the application of shared time programs. While he admitted that not all commentators would agree, he suggested that shared time would offer benefits to both schools and the general community.

January 12, 1965, marked the turning point in the history of shared time education. It was on this day that Lyndon B. Johnson, President of the United States, sent to the 89th Congress his message transmitting his education program. On the same day he had introduced in the House of Representatives

[14] U.S. House of Representatives, *Hearings before the Ad Hoc Subcommittee on Study of Shared Time Education of the Committee on Education and Labor on H.R. 6074*, 88th Congress, 2nd Session, February 24, 25, 28, and March 11, 1964.

[15] " Interfaith Conference Held on Shared Time, " *Boston Pilot* (March 28, 1964), p. 10.

and referred to the Committee on Education and Labor, H.R. 2362, a bill " to strengthen and improve educational quality and educational opportunities in the nation's elementary and secondary schools. " [16]

The President's message and, consequently, the administration's sponsored bill which after approval of Congress was signed into law on April 11, 1965, abandon previous attempts to enact general aid to education by the Federal Government. That approach aimed at large grants of money to State public educational systems, chiefly for construction and for teachers' salaries. However, the exclusion of parochial schools was one, though not the only reason why a general federal aid to elementary and secondary education was never passed by Congress.

The President's education program offered a variety of supplementary and special aids to education. It also made education a factor in the war on poverty. The bill provided for the expenditure of 1.25 billion dollars. The bulk of the money, one billion dollars, fell under Title 1 and was allotted to public school districts in low income areas. School districts became eligible for grants if one hundred of their children or three percent of the children aged five to seventeen came from families with incomes of less than two thousand dollars a year. The bill required that these districts extend to needy paro-

[16] U.S. House of Representatives, H.R. 2362, *A Bill to Strengthen and Improve Educational Quality and Educational Opportunities in the Nation's Elementary and Secondary Schools*, 89 Congress, 1st Session, January 12, 1965, p. 1.

chial and other private school pupils assistance in the
form of dual enrollment or shared service programs.

> A local agency may receive a basic grant or a special
> incentive grant under this title for any fiscal year only
> upon application and therefore approved by the appro-
> priate state educational agency, upon its determination...
> that, to the extent consistent with the number of educa-
> tionally deprived children in the school district of the
> local educational agency who attend nonpublic schools,
> such agency has made provision for including special
> educational services and arrangements (such as dual
> enrollment, educational radio and television, and mobile
> educational services) in which children can participate
> without full-time public school attendance... [17]

Title 2 of H.R. 2362 called for one hundred
million dollars to be used for school library resources
and printed and published instructional materials
for the use of children and teachers in public and
nonprofit private elementary and secondary schools
in the State. Library resources included books,
periodicals, documents, magnetic tapes, phonograph
records and other related library materials while
printed and published instructional materials referred
to charts and textbooks. These library resources
and printed and published instructional materials
must be approved by an appropriate State or local
educational authority for use, or be used in public
elementary or secondary schools of the State. Religious texts were therefore excluded.

Another one hundred million dollars was

[17] *Ibid.*, p. 8.

provided in Title 3 for supplementary educational centers and services. This title aimed to make available the new services and techniques that educational research had developed such as remedial reading, counseling, psychological help, testing programs, educational television, teaching machines, and taped lessons. These educational centers would offer cultural enrichment and special courses to children from both public and Catholic schools.

President Johnson's educational program would vastly change the complex of the American educational scene. Johnson's educational program called for John Doe, student of 1970, to go to a school far different from that attended by his older brothers and sisters. It challenged public and private schools to work together to correct educational weaknesses, most apparent in areas of poverty. Today, slums are educational sore spots, with the oldest buildings, and the fewest textbooks and facilities. The suburbs shine as bright spots of learning with the highest paid, and usually the best teachers and the newest buildings. Under the President's program, the slums would become the new frontiers in education.

Assuming that John Doe is a child from the slums, he would go to a special nursery school to help him overcome any cultural handicaps. In elementary schools he would be given the foundation needed to interest him in learning so that he should not become a school dropout at sixteen.

A typical schoolday might start like this one: 8 : 45 a.m. John would take his place in an attractive classroom where a specially trained teacher would use textbooks about children like himself to teach reading; 9 : 15 a.m. he would work with a tape recorder to improve his speech pattern; 9 : 30 a.m. he would get ready for a field trip to a county courthouse to see government in action. In the afternoon John would go to a well-equipped educational center for science class in up-to-date laboratory. John would be very familiar with the center, for it would also offer counseling services, foreign language laboratories, remedial help and even a quiet place for him to do his homework.

In the center John would also meet children from Catholic schools. One of his friends might be a neighbor, Donald Moran, who begins his school day at the local Catholic school. Donald's schedule might be something like this: opening exercises; history class using the same books as those in use in public schools and supplied by federal funds, but owned by the State; watching a televised class in new mathematics produced and broadcast by the public schools. Then Donald might go to the educational center for an hour in the diagnostic reading clinic. His last class in the afternoon might be in the public school where he would participate in a shared time program, allowing parochial school children to study there part of the day. Donald might take industrial arts in the public school, while other Catholic school students might take home arts or vocational training.

Shared time has both advantages and disadvantages for the Catholic community. The advantages as McDowell sees them are as follows:

1) It would give the parochial school the opportunity to educate effectively all its children. 2) It would assure the community and Catholic parents in this case, that all these children were receiving in major part a religiously-oriented education. 3) It would create new opportunities to achieve a better working relationship between public and parochial school officials and, therefore, as fringe benefits it would eliminate many of the charges that Catholic schools were dropping undesirable students; that they were not melting with the community at the school level; that they were divisive. 4) It would offer the American community an opportunity to maintain private and parochial education through substantial aid given directly to the student and to the public school and, therefore, avoid the distressing conflict of aid to religion debates. 5) It would lessen the tax burden on the total community because it would involve the full use of all existing school buildings and teaching personnel. 6) It would make it possible for the Catholic community to do more at every level, because it would eliminate the excessive cost of erecting gymnasia, language, mathematics, and commercial facilities, and perhaps even cafeterias. [18]

For the Catholic schools then, shared time would provide accommodations for children unable to find seats in crowded classrooms. The staggering costs of new buildings and better facilities would be considerably reduced. By using public schools, Catholic parents would feel that they were getting some return for their taxes. Millions of children in religious schools would now enroll in State schools. This would reduce part of the size of the classes. Parents would pay extra only for religion and those

[18] McDowell, *op. cit.*, p. 22.

subjects directly concerned with values, thus ending double taxation.

In the teaching of subjects in the Catholic schools the teachers could concentrate on becoming experts in what their vocation called them for—the teaching of the Word of God. Under a shared-time system, the need for parochial schools to develop teachers for the secular subjects would be lessened. The parochial schools could then concentrate on the religious and humanistic subjects which they can teach best. At the same time a serious effort could be made to supply an added dimension to key areas of the science curriculum being followed in the public school. The religious teacher could, in connection with a civic course, emphasize the concept of the natural law and natural rights as coming from the Creator. A comparable approach should be possible in most subjects. The possibilities are unlimited.

Perhaps the greatest advantage would be that many children now in public schools would attend some courses in religious schools. Children now receiving little or no formal religious education would begin to receive it in a serious and systematic way. From the Catholic point of view then, over fifty per cent of our children not now in Catholic schools would receive a far better religious education than the one they are getting today.

New vistas would be open for Catholic children. Today, for practical purposes, for all but a very few communities, the Catholic high school is a liberal arts, college preparatory institution. The girl who desires to learn to operate a computer, or the young man whose interest lies in airplane mechanics seldom receives this training at the Catholic high school. These students face the choice of giving up either their career ambitions or their desire for a religious education. Shared time makes such a choice unnecessary by opening up more room for part-time students in parochial schools and at the same time making available the public schools' technical equipment.

For Catholic schools shared time could be infinitely flexible. In some places, the Catholic school might decide to relinquish teaching all laboratory sciences, while retaining a course in the philosophy of science. In other places, the Catholic school could send its students to public schools for physics and chemistry, but might continue to teach biology. In communities with small Catholic populations, the Catholic school at first could teach only a very few courses, leaving possible expansion to a later date. In short, these decisions can be made locally to fit the philosophy and resources of the school administration.

The disadvantages are less serious. There might be grumblings from the Catholic community and from professional educators that a full program is the only answer. There could also be transportation problems, but the working relationship between public and Catholic school officials could be a fringe benefit that would place this disadvantage in the advantage column. There would be of course a problem of records, grading, and other practical administration matters to be faced. The overall disadvantages will be seen in more detail when the problems related to shared time are viewed.

The attitude of American Protestants toward religious education is undergoing a radical change. Protestants can no longer look upon the public schools as institutions of reinforcement for the religious training their children receive at home or at Sunday school. Mail received by members of Congress on prayer and Bible reading reflected the concern of many parents that millions of American children are growing up with no religion. What is not so well known is that since 1940 the growth rate of Protestant parochial day schools has been twice that of Catholic parochial schools and six times that of public schools. The majority of responsible Protestant leaders are opposed to the establishment on a large scale of Protestant system of schools or to a revision of the Constitution which would permit religion in the public schools.

While Catholics are primarily faced with the problem of improving the teaching of secular subjects for children attending parochial schools, the Protestant problem is that of improving religious education for children primarily attending public schools. Under a shared time program Protestants could provide the needed religious training for their children. Protestants would rarely be interested in engaging in as much teaching as Catholics do. Most Protestant parents would be satisfied if their children could take courses in the Bible, theology, Church history, and perhaps Christian philosophy and ethics, and Christian literature and art.

Protestant children could continue to enroll primarily in the public schools but they would have the opportunity to choose courses taught in religious educational foundations. These courses would be taught by teachers appointed and paid by the Churches. Since the courses would be for credit, the teachers and the physical facilities would have to meet State standards, as Catholic schools now do.

The problems for Jewish religious educators are very similar to those of Protestants. However, as a smaller minority group than Catholics, they have even a greater difficulty preserving a distinctive language, culture, and religious tradition. Although there has been a rapid growth recently in Jewish parochial schools, many Jews still turn to the public schools for their education. Under shared time programs, Jewish children who attend public schools could turn to Jewish educational foundations along the same plan outlined for Protestants. Shared time then would enable the Jewish child to study things distinctively Jewish without withdrawing from the public schools.

A second advantage for Jews should be noted. Under released time education, students left the public school to study at religious centers. This often meant that all the " religious " children left for released time classes while the " irreligious or non-religious " children remained in school. Jewish leaders felt that this caused friction and religious bias, and many of them opposed released time because of this factor. However, in developed shared time programs, students from parochial schools would be entering the public schools at various times during the day and the classes held at the religious centers could be so arranged that at no time would the non-participating students be isolated in the public schools.

For Catholics, Protestants, and Jews, taken separately, the advantages of shared time education are incalculable. For all three, the advantages of bringing children of different beliefs together would be combined with the advantages of separate sectarian instruction. Stearns sums up well the sentiments of many non-Catholics when he writes:

> There is great urgency to this matter. The present trend of affairs, breeding divisiveness and distrust, and the undermining of our school system at a time when its potency is sorely needed cannot continue if our free Westen civilization and our Judeo-Christian tradition are to survive. The situation is critical. If sharing of time will offer a solution for those who want religious education at the hands of the Church and at the same time will preserve the separation of Church and State, it is worthy of full exploration.
>
> It is reasonable to assume that if Roman Catholic, Protestant and Jewish leardership can unite on the basic validity of shared time, many communities may be found where the goodwill of the citizens and the ingenuity of the school leadership may be utilized to demonstrate that the concept can be made to work for the benefit of all. [19]

Shared time education is not without its advantages for the public schools. Parents of children attending Catholic schools would be more inclined to support increased budgets for public

[19] Stearns, *Shared Time—a Symposium*, p. 10.

schools if their own children received some of the
benefits through part-time attendance. This would
relieve some of the feelings of injustice about the
present distribution of educational funds. As Msgr.
Arthur T. Geoghegan, Superintendent of Catholic
schools, Diocese of Providence, Rhode Island,
states:

> It would seem that the best interests of the Nation
> and the community would be served by shared time.
> The financial burden of supporting public and Church-
> related schools currently borne by those who attend the
> latter would be substantially alleviated. The public-aid-
> to-the Church-schools controversy should then diminish
> or disappear, and the increased taxes and bond issues to
> expand and improve public school education would
> receive more general and less grudging support. [20]

Shared time then would give the whole community a stake in the budget and the quality of the
public schools.

Another important advantage would be that
while shared time would lead to more intensified
religious education, it would decrease religious
segregation since almost all students would spend
some time together in the public schools. Because
of the mixing of students, groups which maintain
private schools to foster racial or class separation
would be unable to take advantage of shared time.
The Black Muslim and white supremacy philosophies
would be excluded. Although shared time offers
diversity in education, it still preserves integration
of the whole educational effort.

[20] *Ibid.*, p. 24.

An additional advantage of the program for public schools is the better use of expensive educational equipment. The revolution in space and technology has been joined by a revolution in education. New educational equipment often becomes outmoded in five years. It may prove more efficient in the future to build central school libraries, laboratories, shops and certain physical educational facilities, which can be comprehensive, serviced by trained personnel and used by all students, than to scatter inadequate units around the city.

Endorsements and signs of interest in shared time have come from many directions. From the Catholic side Lawrence Cardinal Shehan of Baltimore looks upon shared time with enthusiastic interest. Bishop Stephen S. Woznicki of Saginaw, Michigan, has said of shared time that " it's the best solution I've seen. " [21]   Catholic school administrators in Pittsburgh, Philadelphia, Chicago, and Detroit are either initiating or expanding shared time programs.

In 1964, appearing before a Congressional subcommittee on H.R. 6074, Msgr. Frederick G. Hochwalt, then the Director of Education for the National Catholic Welfare Conference, testified that shared time could be a possible step or partial solution toward the pursuit of excellence in education. [22]   In January 1965, commenting on President

[21] Maurine Hoffman, " Detroit Suburb Tries Shared Time, " *Washington Post* (February 24, 1964), p. 5.

[22] U.S. House of Representatives, *Hearings on H.R. 6074*, pp. 261-82.

Johnson's program for education as contained in H.R. 2362, Hochwalt said:

> The major purpose of the President's message is to meet the educational needs of the children. This emphasis on the child, the student, I applaud.
>
> Priority is given to children in areas of economic distress. This is as it should be. Improving educational opportunities in areas of proven need will best profit both the child and the nation. I would urge, however, that consideration be given to other resources available in those areas, namely, the private non-profit schools. It should be emphasized repeatedly that the beneficiaries of any aid program should be the child wherever his wants are found.
>
> Of great significance is the fact that the President calls for cooperation between the nation's public and private schools. I have always considered the public and private school systems of this country to be partners, not competitors, in education. Our experience in many parts of the country proves the great benefit that such a partnership can be to the children in all schools. The Administration's suggestion to extend that partnership poses a new challenge for educators. [23]

Testifying on the President's bill before a subcommittee, Hochwalt proposed that to carry out the intent of the legislation, some form of consultation should be required between authorities of the public and private systems on the types of programs to be offered and the books to be provided. [24]

---

[23] " Education Proposals to Get Prompt Action, " *Washington Catholic Standard*, XV (February 5, 1965), p. 1.

[24] John J. Daly, " Religious Spokesmen Back School Aid Plan, " *Washington Catholic Standard*, XV (February 5, 1965), p. 1.

Bishop William E. McManus, Superintendent of Schools of the Archdiocese of Chicago, has been an early advocate of shared time. The Bishop heads a school system of nearly 365,000 pupils, a total topped in the country only by the public school systems of New York, Los Angeles, and Chicago itself. Endorsing the aspects of shared time in the President's program, McManus expressed the hope that for order in the parochial schools, trained teachers from the public schools might be able to come to private schools to give special courses to children in need of specialized attention. However, this was an administrative problem and if any questions arose concerning the procedure, Catholic parents would take the children to where they would be given the class. McManus considered the Administration's program a compromise in the controversy concerning Church and State, but like all compromises the program would not please all parties.

There is no consensus among the diocesan superintendents of schools on the subject of shared time. In a 1967 educational survey conducted by the publication *U.S. Catholic*, only twenty-eight of the fifty-two superintendents queried favored shared time at the elementary level. Thirty-four of the fifty-two superintendents were in favor of shared time at the high school level. [25]

James O'Gara, a Catholic layman, has devoted several of his columns in *Commonweal* to shared time, finding much to commend in the program. O'Gara

[25] Educational Survey of Diocesan Superintendents, " *U.S. Catholic* (April, 1967), pp. 13-14.

has been critical of Catholics as well as non-Catholics who would write off shared time before having given it a real chance. [26]

On the Protestant and Orthodox side the National Council of Churches which represents thirty-four denominations and forty million members through its one hundred and twenty member policy-making general board has endorsed experiments in shared time.

> It is our hope that dual school enrollment may prove to be a means of helping our nation to maintain the values of a general system of public education, yet at the same time meeting the needs of those who desire a system of Church-related education, while upholding the historic American principle of separation and interaction of Church and State. [27]

On May 26th, 1964, the General Assembly of the United Presbyterian Church stated that in principle it supported shared time. Dr. Dumont F. Kenny, Vice-president of the National Conference of Christians and Jews, is said to have called shared time " the most promising idea on the horizon to assist American communities in providing an adequate program of education, both secular and religious. " [28]

Arthur Flemming, First Vice-President of the National Council of Churches and Secretary of

[26] James O'Gara, " A Chance for Shared Time, " *Commonweal*, LXXX (April 17, 1964), p. 110.

[27] " Protestant Group Backs Shared Time Education, " *Boston Pilot* (June 13, 1964), p. 11.

[28] Research Division—National Education Association, 1964, *op. cit.*, p. 15.

Health, Education and Welfare in the Eisenhower Administration, was one of the early advocates of shared time as a possible solution to the Church-State conflict in education. Writing about the difficulties which would have to be overcome, Flemming recognized the existence of barriers, " ... but I do not believe they are insurmountable. The cooperative planning that would be required to eliminate them would not only strengthen the total educational program of the community but would introduce a unifying force in the life of the community. "[29]

The feelings of many non-Catholic supporters of shared time could well be summarized in the words of the Reverend Dean Kelley of the National Council of Churches Commission on Religious Liberty. " Support of the bill (Johnson's program for education) is a calculated risk. It requires an act of confidence that we can work out a fair solution, and the demonstration that we are no longer afraid of each other. "[30]

On the Jewish side support for shared time has come from the Jewish Orthodox congregations and rabbis, the Society for Hebrew Schools, and the liberal American Jewish Committee. Rabbi Marc Tanenbaum, Director of the American Jewish Committee's Department of Interreligious Affairs, believes that " if the so-called Catholic absolutists are

[29] Arthur Flemming, " The Shared Time Program Is Worth A Try, " *Good Housekeeping*, CLVI (February, 1963), p. 52.

[30] " What Price Partnership? " *Newsweek* (February 22), 1965, p. 59.

prepared to risk testing their truth in a heteroge-
neous school system with its pluralistic values, I
should think that the relativists and pragmatists
would be equally prepared to experiment before
they close the door on the proposals. " [31]

An Orthodox Jewish spokesman, Rabbi Morris
Sherer of Agudath Israel of America, appearing
before the House Committee on Education supported shared time and called it a major step in meeting
the educational needs of school children. Rabbi
Sherer was gratified that the needs of children in
religious schools were not ignored. The rabbi noted
that Orthodox Jews now have three hundred schools
in more than one hundred cities. The fact that
children in these and other Church-related schools
would share some benefits with public school pupils
means an enrichment of our country's potential in
fulfilling our national purpose.

The impression must not be given that all
Protestant and Jews accept shared time. The National Association of Evangelicals, representing
more than two and a half million largely fundamen-
talist Christians as well as the Unitarian Universalist
Association have opposed shared time. The American Jewish Congress, the Anti-Defamation League
of B'nai B'rith and the representatives of Reform
Judaism suspect shared time. Most opposition
stems from problems of Church-State or of administration and will be investigated in more detail in a
review of the problems related to shared time.

On the secular scene the *New Republic* saw

[31] *Ibid.*

shared time as a very hopeful sign of compromise without sacrifice of principles.

> Not a stone in the wall of separation is dislodged... and anything that gives the whole community a vested interest in better education is to the good. Giving Catholic parents a direct investment in the public as well as the parochial schools surely ought to make it easier to win community support for school bonds.... [32]

Senator Abraham Ribicoff of Connecticut, Secretary of Health, Education, and Welfare in the early years of the Kennedy Administration, has argued that a combination of his proposals on shared time and tax deductions for parents of children attending private schools can resolve the religious controversy in education. Francis Keppel, former Dean of the School of Education at Harvard University, when he was United States Commissioner of Education, in an address to the AFL-CIO legislative conference viewed shared services between public and parochial schools as expanding educational opportunities for all children, thus improving the overall educational system and at the same time avoiding the Church-State controversy.

Perhaps the finest support for shared time has come from public school superintendents who have programs in their schools. Superintendents with known shared time programs received question-naires from the Research Division of the National Education Association. Replies from 183 superin-tendents indicated acceptance of valid dual school

[32] *New Republic*, XXLVIII (May 11, 1964), pp. 4-6.

enrollment programs. To the question, " In the light of your experience, would you advise other school districts to provide a program of shared time? " 63 percent answered, " Yes, " 9 percent said " No, " and 28 percent did not answer.

> Most superintendents qualified their answer. For example, one superintendent said, " This would depend on the individual classes, and the willingness of the individual teachers to take on extra students. " [33]

The two leading organizations of public school educators have endorsed shared time programs. The National Education Association, which in the past traditionally opposed federal aid programs to private and parochial schools, voiced its approval of the Johnson program. In February 1965, the American Association of School Administrators at the end of its annual meeting in Atlantic City issued the following statement:

> The Association also believes that common educational experiences, which are shared by persons of all faiths, contribute to the strengthening of our nation and that it is therefore in the public interest to make available to all children and teachers the library resources and published educational materials which will contribute to this goal. [34]

This was a major shift in the organization's position on relations between private and parochial schools.

The emphasis on shared time and other

[33] Research Division—National Education Association, 1964, *op. cit.*, pp. 8-9.
[34] Gerald Grant, " Superintendents Back School Aid Bill, " *Washington Post* (February 18, 1965), p. 4.

cooperation between public and private schools had been one of the major themes of this convention. Speakers who had questioned the constitutionality of non-public school aid were applauded vigorously. However, it was clear that the leadership of the Association and the superintendents from the large cities were behind the program. The resolution was approved without dissent by the 800 superintendents present.

Endorsement and enthusiastic interest in shared time have come from many directions. Support has been manifested by religious leaders, Catholics, Protestants, and Jews, by secular sources, and by politicians and educators. Msgr. Arthur T. Geoghegan's realistic summary of the program reflects the attitudes of its leading advocates.

> Shared time is no panacea. It will not cure all the the problems concerned with religion in education. But by enabling a pupil to share in the complementary strengths of the public and Church-sponsored schools alike, it offers the best promise to date of providing for the religious dimension in the education of most of our children. [35]

[35] Arthur T. Geoghegan, " Shared Time Plan Favored, " *Catholic Educator*, XXXII (June, 1962), p. 913.

The Church and the State

Fundamental to both a theoretical understanding and a practical application of shared time education is a proper grasp of the general relationship that should exist between the Church and the State. Unfortunately, the relationship of these two great institutions of Western culture has been one of the ever recurring problems of political history.

The practical problems involved in the relationship between Church and State in the United States have in recent years become burning political issues. Church-State relations were a significant factor in the presidential campaign of 1960. They are a major issue in the dispute over federal aid to private and parochial schools. They were involved in the Supreme Court decisions where the recitation of a State-composed prayer in public schools was declared unconstitutional, and in the cases concerning compulsory Bible reading and recitation of the Lord's Prayer in public schools. In recent months conflict has arisen over laws concerning censorship, abortion, and the tax exemption of Church property.

Practical problems, especially those regarding education, will rise from time to time and are worthy of consideration. However, more important is a proper understanding of the principles of right relationship between the Church and the State. Principles do not carry with themselves solutions to practical problems. Nevertheless, practical difficulties can be settled only in the light of correct principles. It is essential for a study of shared time to consider then the Catholic position on the proper relationship between Church and State.

In a theoretical discipline such as theology abstract principles are accepted because of consistency. It should not be expected that practical problems in a concrete context can be solved with simple affirmations or simple negations. As the ate Gustave Weigel wrote:

> This is impossible. A theological answer is in the abstract order in which different hypotheses must be considered. The expression of the hypotheses may sound to the lay hearer as elegant evasion or lack of candor. It is neither. The theologian can do nothing else and still be a theologian. Two and three can be mathematically related to each other as two-thirds, one, minus one, five or six, depending on the operation to be performed. [1]

There are many approaches which could be taken to arrive at a proper understanding of the relationship between the Church and the State. For the most part, our investigation will be limited to an examination of the thoughts of two contemporary American theologians, the late John Courtney Murray and his colleague for many years at the

[1] Gustave Weigel, *Church-State Relations—A Theological Consideration* (Baltimore: Helicon, 1960), p. 4.

Jesuit School of Divinity in Woodstock, Maryland, Gustave Weigel. This limitation is indicated because the concepts of these two men are most relevant to the problems and experiences of this country and appear to be in full agreement with the American tradition of freedom of conscience in a pluralistic society. At the same time the thoughts of Murray and Weigel demonstrate an essential conformity with the mind of the Fathers of Vatican II as represented in the Declaration on Religious Freedom.

It is necessary to note that the Church has never made, and probably will never make, a dogmatic statement on the relationship which should exist between the Church and the State. The area is open to free theological opinion and discussion. There is no theological thesis of the relations of Church and State. The political-ethical theses which have been maintained, and some of which have become conventional, are based on the historical acts of the Church, theoretically justified by philosophical reasoning.

Perhaps the difficulty involved in formulating a dogmatic statement is the silence of the New Testament. There are no concrete principles expressed of what the relationship between the Church and the State should be.

The New Testament did not arise in a vacuum, for its origins are in Judaism and the Old Testament. " The Old Testament knows only two States: the monarchies of Israel and Judah in one group, and all other States together. Israel is submitted to God; all other States are not in submission. " [2]

The concrete historical situation of the New Testament must also be considered. There is no consideration of the State in the abstract. The only State it knows is Rome; and Rome was a superstate, effectively a world State. Therefore, the only relations between the Church and the State is one of an attitude, the attitude toward Rome.

If we were to investigate the sayings of Jesus or even the writings of Paul, there is not the slightest indication that the State was conceived as having anyformal relations to the Church. At most we would find the concept that " the Christian must live in the State, and he must live in it as a Christian. " [3]

With no theology of Church and State set forth in Scripture, theologians have worked within their national framework to develop general principles which would govern the relationship between the two great institutions which often found themselves in disagreement. With the establishment of the United States new problems were set forth for the Church by the uniqueness of the American social situation, by the genius of the newly conceived constitutional system, and by the lessons of its singular national history. All of these have " molded in a special way the consciousness and temper of

[2] John L. McKenzie, " The State in Christian Perspective, " *Critic*, XXII (June-July, 1964), p. 16.

[3] *Ibid.*, p. 21.

the American people within whose midst the Catholic stands, sharing with his fellow citizens the American national heritage. " [4]

It is no wonder then that in the early days of the founding of the American Republic Rome could not fully comprehend the unique relationship that would exist between the Church and the government. In 1783, the Papal nuncio to Paris sent a note to Benjamin Franklin informing him that the Holy See was considering removing the American Catholics from the jurisdiction of the Vicar Apostolic in London and was going to appoint a resident bishop in the United States. Franklin directed the communication to the Continental Congress. The reply was forwarded to Franklin that he was to inform Rome that the matter of appointing a bishop was a purely spiritual affair and outside the jurisdiction of the government.

No American theologian has ever claimed that the Catholic way of life makes it impossible to accept the Constitution, to swear to maintain it, and to lay down one's life to defend it. Catholics in the United States need not feel a conflict in conscience between their democratic allegiance and their Catholic commitment. [5]

The American political system involves freedom of conscience, freedom of speech, and freedom of worship for all Americans, without help or hindrance

[4] John Courtney Murray, " The Problem of Pluralism in America, " *Thought*, XXIX (Summer 1954), p. 166.

[5] Gustave Weigel, " The Church and the Democratic State, " *Thought*, XXVII (Summer 1952), p. 167.

from the government which by the Constitution is deprived of the power to deal with the religious affairs of the land.   The result is that there can be no established State Church, nor favor nor vexation of any religious or irreligious group.   As a result the State as a political unit makes no religious profession implying adhesion to one of the many churches in its midst.

The Church has benefited in the United States, even by exaggerated forms of distinctions between Church and State.   By accepting this relationship, the Church has committed itself to peace in a pluralistic society.

The relationship between Church and State in the United States was and is unique.   Although the countries of Western Europe, especially France, claimed liberal tradition and relations between the government and the Church, the so-called free Church was subject to political control more complete than the Tudor, Stuart, or Bourbon rulers ever dreamed of.   This was evidenced in France during the period from the Civil Constitution of the Clergy in 1790, to the Law of Separation in 1905.   The State pretended to ignore the Church, yet never took more cognizance of it.

The view of ignoring, yet controlling the Church, developed into a denial of any rights for the religious order as is witnessed in the totalitarian people's democracies behind the Iron Curtain.   For those who deny a sacral or sacred order, or affirm that it is only a phase of the secular, there are no problems between the Church and the State.   Only two things can be related to each other. If there is only the State, no relations can exist. [6]

In formulating principles between Church and State Murray and Weigel feel that certain distinctions must be maintained. The first is the distinction between the sacral or religious order, and the secular, or temporal order. " Now the sacral order is the plane, or better, the dimension of man's relationship to divinity and the secular order is the dimension of man's relationship to the world of finite realities, especially to the fellow man with whom he lives. " [7]

Man exists for a transcendent end. The whole of his existence is not absorbed in the temporal and terrestrial. The power of the State does not reach into this higher sacred order of human existence. It has no share in the *cura animarum* or in the *regimen animorum*. [8] As Murray writes:

> It (the State) is not the judge or the representative of transcendent truth with regard to man's eternal destiny; it is not man's guide to heaven. Its powers are limited to the affairs of the temporal and terrestrial order of man's existence. And they are not to be used as instruments for the spiritual purposes of the Church—the maintenance of her unity or the furtherance of her mission. [9]

[6] Gustave Weigel, *Church-State Relations—A Theological Consideration*, p. 4.

[7] *Ibid.*, p. 5.

[8] Leo XIII, " Sapientiae Christianae, " *Acta Sanctae Sedis*, XXII (1889-90), p. 396. Leo XIII made it quite clear that political authority has no part whatsoever in the care of souls *(cura animarum)* or in the control of the minds of men *(regimen animorum)*.

[9] John Courtney Murray, " The Problem of Religious Freedom, " *Theological Studies*, XXV (December, 1964), p. 520.

A second distinction should be made between society and the State. Historically, this developed out of the medieval distinction between *ecclesia* (*christianitas*) and the imperium. [10] The imperial power had a limited role to play within Christendom. Today in countries with a constitutional tradition the State is an agency that plays a limited role within society. Again quoting from Murray:

> The purposes of the State are not coextensive with the purposes of society. The State is only one order within society—the order of public law and political administration. The public powers, which are invested with the power of the State, are charged with the performance of certain limited functions for the benefit of society—such functions as can and must be performed by the coercive discipline of law and political power. These functions are defined by constitutional law, in accord with the consent of the people. In general " society " signifies an area of freedom, personal and corporate, whereas " State " signifies the area in which the public powers may legitimately apply their coercive powers. To deny the distinction is to espouse the notion of government as totalitarian. [11]

To identify State and society, and State and government is the essence of totalitarianism.

From the distinction between society and the State there flows another between common good and public order. " The common good includes all the social goods, spiritual and moral as well as material, which man pursues here on earth in accord with the demands of his personal and social

[10] *Ibid.*
[11] *Ibid.*

nature. " [12]   Society as a whole with all its members and institutions, is involved with the pursuit of the common good, taking into account the principles of subsidiarity, legal justice, and distributive justice. On the other hand the State is involved with the public order.   Murray views the public order as a much narrower concept than that of the common good:

> It (public order) includes three goods which can and should be achieved by the power which is proper to the State—the power inherent in the coercive discipline of public law. The first is the public peace, which is the highest political good. The second is public morality, as determined by moral standards commonly accepted among the people. The third is justice, which secures for the people what is due to them. And the first thing that is due to the people, in justice, is their freedom, the due enjoyment of their personal and social rights—those empowerments and immunities to which the people, individually, collectively, and corporatively, lay rightful claim. [13]

With these distinctions in mind three general basic principles governing Church and State as formulated by John Courtney Murray and Gustave Weigel may now be cited.

> (1) The sacral order, distinct as it is from the order of the secular, is a superior order. Its claims are absolute and its imperatives unconditional. The secular order cannot legitimately make demands if its demands go counter to those which are sacral. [14]

[12] *Ibid.*
[13] *Ibid.*, pp. 520-21.
[14] Weigel, *Church-State Relations—A Theological Consideration*, pp. 5-6.

This principle is fundamental to Catholic theology and is commoly accepted by mankind at large. In most general terms it is referred to as the principle of the inviolability of conscience. " Even the Church, which has authority to oblige conscience, has no power to coerce it. " No State has the power to coerce the conscience of man to any form of belief or unbelief, or to judge whether a conscience is true or erroneous. [15]

To comprehend ecclesial freedom as proposed in the principle, it is necessary to understand something of the nature of the Church. The Church is above all a spiritual authority which derives rights from a direct commission from Christ without any dependence upon human institutions and without any fear of interference in its spiritual authority by an institution other than its own constituted hierarchy. As a juridical institution the Church has an internal order of law and is capable, as are other juridical institutions, of solving and treating internal problems. The Church then is a community of the faithful, a visible society with members open to all under certain membership qualifications.

The Church then is *sui juris*, distinct from civil society in origin, constitution, purpose and transcending all political forms. There exists the right to define its own status of existence on the basis of the divine will, to determine forms of organization and government and norms of ecclesial life and action, and to elect or appoint rulers, to educate the

[15] Murra,   y*The Problem of Religious Freedom,* pp. 523-24.

clergy, and to communicate across national boundaries. In internal affairs the Church is free from interference by the State whose powers are limited to the purposes and interest of the body politic which concerns itself with civil affairs. " Internal ecclesiastical affairs are no more the concern of the public powers than the affairs of the internal forum of conscience. " [16]

The Erastian teaching that the public powers are the arbiter of religious truths and the architect of Church polity is contrary to Christian doctrine. Civil law has no power to coerce the religious conscience or the social expression of religious conscience. The care of religion, since it implies the care of souls, is not a function of the State. The care of religion devolves upon those institutions whose purposes are religious—the Church and the churches, and various voluntary associations for religious purposes. The care of religion, " in so far as it is a duty incumbent on the State, is limited to a care for the religious freedom of the body politic. " [17] The Church alone then has exclusive right over spiritual things both within herself and within the temporal order.

(2) Catholic theology holds that in the matter of the relations between sacral and secular the civic community, and therefore its State, are necessary God-willed institutions.... The concerns of the natural order must be referred to the laws of the State as guide and norm. The State is naturally competent to deal with such matters

[16] *Ibid.,* p. 524.
[17] *Ibid.,* p. 528.

and it is autonomous, free and authoritative in its decisions. There is no natural institution over the State, even though there is a higher human order, the sacral, which is on an altogether different level. On its own level of natural concern, the State is man's highest social institution. Nor need the State be exclusively national; it can take on international characteristics as well. [18]

This second principle is no less important than the first, though it is subordinate. Man as a civic animal must coexist and collaborate with others. The highest pattern of social coexistence is called civil society and the " mode of societal structure it adopts is called the State. " [19] The state is a polity and there can be many kinds of polities. Some states are monarchic; others are oligarchic, while others are democratic.

States are natural things since their origins are in human nature. They are therefore non-sacral. This does not imply that the State is not under God. Like all other creatures the State is subject to the divine will. However, the State is concerned with the temporal welfare of its members and is not religious in its preoccupations. It looks manwards and not Godwards. Laws are made by the State in consideration of the human situation and there must be a toleration of all the defects inherent in this situation. Weigel describes the function of the State in the following way:

[18] Weigel, *Church-State Relations—A Theological Consideration*, pp. 7-8.

[19] *Ibid.*, p. 7.

The laws of God are absolute directions for man but the State makes its laws relative to the human predicament and relative to the common good of all citizens. Divine law and human law are of quite different textures. God's law may forbid this or that action but the State may wisely permit it, lest greater evil fall upon the community. The State wants to keep the community together almost at all costs because this is its only interest and concern. The State is not God and its will is not ultimate nor absolute. [20]

Human law then exists for the human community and is neither a religious profession of faith nor a promulgation of divine law. It is conceivable that human law could banish certain theoretically immoral things yet in the concrete disrupt the community because the fulfilling of the law through wide police interference into the private lives of the people might make life intolerable. "Human law is for the natural common good of all, and no laws should be made which are not necessary for that common good. " [21]

The Catholic man of State should strive to enact laws for the common good of his concrete community according to its unique history and character. For the legislator there must be an awareness that the function of civil law is not to teach theology or maintain even the moral views of the framer of the law. Whether the legislator be Catholic, Protestant, or Jew it would be immoral to impose upon the community what he thinks is immoral. Acceptance of immorality, if demanded

[20] *Ibid.*
[21] *Ibid.*, p. 11.

by the common good is " good law and in accord with the morality of political action. " [22]

The Catholic statesman comes to his office with a Catholic conscience, just as a Protestant statesman comes with a Protestant conscience. Neither comes to fulfill the office of moral teacher or moral philosopher. This does not imply that the attempt to impose one moral theory or another is not the function of the statesman. Weigel considers the man of State a citizen with a double life:

> He has his own and that of a civil servant. If in his own life he wishes to worship in one way or in none, this is no political concern of the civic community. By our laws he is free in the matter. In his public role he is a man of the law which is framed for practical purposes and canonizes no philosophy or theology. I can conceive of a highly moral man who in his interior conscience considers traffic in liquor to be immoral and yet could refuse to make a law about it, or even vote for the removal of such existing legislation. He is being highly moral in his political action if he judges that such a law would do more public harm than good. [23]

Jacques Maritain accepts the above view when he writes:

> ... that the legislation of the Christian society in question could and should never endorse or approve any way of conduct contrary to natural law. But we have also to realize that this legislation could and should permit or give allowance to certain ways of conduct which depart in some measure from natural law, if the prohibition by civil law of these ways of conduct were

[22] *Ibid.*, p. 14.
[23] *Ibid.*, p. 15.

to impair the common good, either because such prohibition would be at variance with the ethical code of communities of citizens whose loyalty to the nation and faithfulness to their own moral creed, however imperfect it may be, essentially matter to the common good, or even because it would result in a worse conduct, disturbing or disintegrating the social body, for a great many people whose moral strength is not on a level with the enforcement of this prohibition. [24]

Civil legislation then should adapt itself to a variety of moral beliefs because of the diverse spiritual, and even non-spiritual lineage of the people, not by endorsing them or approving of them, but rather by giving allowance to them. This concept is essential in a pluralistic State in which all forms of worship and moral behavior need to be accepted for the sake of the common good.

(3) The third Catholic principle on the relations between Church and State is that in this quite un-ideal world Church and State should strive after the closest concretely possible approximination to an ideal concord, which nevertheless never means identity. [25]

According to Catholic theology man is subject to two directives and two imperatives. One is absolute and that is the sacral; the other is relative and it is the secular.

Man belongs to two orders and is therefore subject to both. Conflict between the two orders

[24] Jacques Maritain, *Man and the State* (Chicago: University of Chicago Press, 1951), pp. 167-68.

[25] Weigel, *Church-State Relations—A Theological Consideration*, p. 8.

need not arise since the Church and the State are God-willed. This State, since it functions according to the dictates of nature which is divinely structured, will be no obstacle to man's sacral imperatives. In the ideal there is a pre-established concord between the Church and State.

The Church is to cooperate with the State, and the State is to cooperate with the Church. Each acts towards its own distinct end, which is ultimate in its own order; but since these two ends, temporal and spiritual, are ordered ends of man, the operations of Church and State must be ordered into a cooperation, to the end that the ordered good of man may be achieved.

Out of necessity then there should be an orderly relation between the two powers since the rule of both is over the same person. If therefore there is no harmony between them, the conflict is felt in the depths of the personal conscience, which knows itself to be obliged to both of the powers which are from God. Harmony is required by the unity and integrity of the human personality. The theological dictum of the fifth-century Pope, Gelasius I, could well summarize the individual's relations to both orders, *civis idem et christianus*, the same one man who is a citizen is also a Christian.

Although there is a principle of contact and mutual cooperation, the Catholic position is not one of union or establishment. At the same time the suppression of any actual contact and connection, of any mutual help, between the Church and the body politic would simply spell suicide. For

Maritain cooperation is of the very essence of democracy:

> Moreover the common good itself of the temporal society implies that human persons are indirectly assisted by the latter in their movement toward supra-temporal achievement, which is an essential part of the pursuit of happiness. Finally (not to speak even of the fact, defined by theology, that human nature in its existential condition needs divine grace in order to achieve its highest human ends, social as well as individual), the Christian political society... would be aware of the fact that Christian truths and incentives and the inspiration of the Gospel, awakening common consciousness and passing into the sphere of temporal existence, are the very soul, inner strength, and spiritual stronghold of democracy. Just as democracy must, under penalty of disintegration, foster and defend the democratic charter, so a Christian democracy, that is a democracy fully aware of its own sources, must, under penalty of disintegration, keep alive in itself the Christian sense of human dignity and human equality, of justice and freedom. [26]

There are two specific forms by which mutual assistance may take place. The first, and most basic, is the recognition and guarantee by the State of the freedom of the Church. Recognition of this freedom is required because the Church and its members have a God-given right to fulfill their sacral missions. Freedom of the Church does not imply ignorance of the Church nor does it imply granting special juridical privileges to those citizens who are members of the sacral order.

There is a second form of required mutual

[26] Maritain, *op. cit.*, pp. 176-77.

assistance. It is not merely a negative assistance as is the insurance of freedom, but a positive one, which in no way infringes upon the basic rule of equal laws and equal rights for all citizens. In this case the State asks the Church for assistance and cooperation in the field of all activities which aim at enlightening human minds and life. The State should positively facilitate the religious, social, and educational work by means of which the Church, as well as other spiritual or cultural groups, whose help for the common good would be recognized by the State, freely cooperate in the common welfare. By removing obstacles and opening the doors, the body politic, its free agencies and institutions, would positively facilitate the effort of the apostles of the Gospel to go to the masses and share their life, to assist the social and moral work of the nation, to provide people with leisure worthy of human dignity, and to develop within them the sense of liberty and fraternity.

For the Catholic, just as for every other member of society, the human person must have an effect upon temporal order that is the State. The Catholic cannot jettison his Catholicism; quite the contrary, he has the positive obligation to have a Christian influence upon the society of which he is a member and upon the State and government of that society. The Christian has to be a constructive member of a democratic society.

This concept is paramount since the rise of democracies has brought about new methods of contact between the Church and the State. In a pluralistic society such as exists in the United States fruitful communication between the State and the Church does not often take place. The Church as a church is not capable of influencing directly the temporal order. The problem falls upon the civic person in the world who through the medium of democratic institutions brings concord and harmony to the Church and the State.

The reconciliation of the two distinct institutions occurs where the obligation to both societies begins, in the individual. Harmony exists for the person, but it is the same person who by his activity as a Christian and as a citizen accomplishes concord between the Church and the State. Thus the problem of the Church's role in the temporal order is placed in the hands of the single individual. In some cases the Church's purposes may collide with those of the State and vice versa. Where problems arise in a democratic society the implications of Christianity are mediated to the State through the individual citizen. In this fashion the entire problem returns to its starting point, the freedom of the Church and the individual human person in society.

In considering the principle of cooperation and from what has been written explaining the other two principles certain points of clarification have emerged. The first is that the natural State operates only in terms of human law, considering always the public order. The second is that the concept of the State must be constantly revised in the light of what modern States really are. The Church in basic form remains the same, no matter what the culture, period of time or State may be; but the State itself takes on various forms and even in the course of time a particular form of the State may change. Finally, it must be remembered that " geometrical positions of abstract thought are not meant to be blue prints for concrete structures. " [27] Applications of abstract principles must take into consideration concrete existential situations.

The similarity between these principles and the American practice should be evident. For the First Amendment, in making nonestablishment a legal requirement, puts the question of harmony upon the individual. The Amendment recognized the diversity of religious and even irreligious beliefs of the people. Implicit is the recognition that the government is limited and certain areas are not the immediate concern of the State.

The First Amendment is not a theological but a political document; it is not an answer to theological problems, nor is it a dogma of Catholic and Protestant ecclesiology. The First Amendment very simply recognizes the limitations of the State in the realm of religion and human conscience. There is an open distinction made between the Church and the State. Therefore, the First Amendment must be looked at not as religious dogma but as law. A rather long quote from John Courtney Murray can set the Amendment in its proper framework:

[27] Weigel, *Church-State Relations—A Theological Consideration*, p. 11.

We should, therefore, make some advance toward clarity if we could all agree to take the First Amendment exactly for what it is—not a theological, but a political document. It does not define a concept of the Church but a concept of the State. Fundamentally, the First Amendment asserts that political sovereignty is limited by the rights of conscience inherent in man. It has simply an ethical and a political content. Its ethical content is the doctrine that religious conscience is immune from governmental coercion. And its political content is the assertion that the rights of conscience will be most securely protected and the political ends of the American State most effectively furthered by guaranteeing the equality of all religious consciences (and by implication, of all religious bodies) before the law. It cannot be too much emphasized that the religious liberty proclaimed by the First Amendment is not a piece of religious mysticism, but a practical political principle, ethically grounded on the obligations of the State to the consensus of its citizens and its own ends—social harmony, prosperity, and peace. [28]

No formal document on the relations between the Church and State issued from Vatican II. However, two documents did make certain significant contributions toward a development of doctrine in regard to the Church-State issue, the Declaration on Religious Freedom and the Constitution on the Church in the Modern World.

Vatican II did not limit itself merely to the problems of the Church. Aware of the signs of the times, namely the rising consciousness of the dignity of the human person and the mounting movement

[28] John Courtney Murray, " Separation of Church and State, " *America*, LXXVI (December 7, 1946), p. 261.

toward the unity of the human family, the Fathers of the Council concerned themselves with the universal human right, freedom of conscience. Taking their cue from John XXIII in *Pacem in Terris* that " every human being has the right to honor God according to the dictates of an upright conscience, and therefore the right to worship God privately and publicly, " [29] the Fathers viewed government as " constitutional and as limited in function—its primary function being juridical, namely, the protection and promotion of the rights of man and the facilitation of the performance of man's native duties. " [30]

The Declaration disavows the long-standing view that the government has a sacral function, namely to defend and promote religious truths. The function of government appears as the protection and promotion, not of religious truth, but of religious freedom as a fundamental right of the human person.

> Therefore, government is to assume the safeguard of the religious freedom of all its citizens, in an effective manner, by just laws and by other appropriate means. Government is also to help create conditions favorable to the fostering of religious life, in order that the people may be truly enabled to exercise their religious rights and to fulfill their religious duties, and also in order that society itself may profit by the moral qualities of justice

[29] John XXIII, *Pacem in Terris* (Boston: St. Paul Edition, 1964), p. 9.

[30] John Courtney Murray, " The Issue of Church and State at Vatican Council II, " *Theological Studies*, XXVII (December, 1966), p. 586.

and peace which have their origin in men's faithfulness to God and to His holy will. [31]

This function then of government is secular " since freedom in society—notably religious freedom—is a secular value, as are the values of justice and love or civic friendship. " [32]

In systematic harmony with its own doctrine on the universal right to religious freedom and the limitations of governmental power in matters religious, the Declaration makes the statement: " The freedom of the Church is the fundamental principle in what concerns the relations between the Church and governments and the whole civil order. " [33] Freedom of the Church implies her necessary independence in the fulfillment of her divine mission. The Church claims freedom as an authority and as a community. Therefore, the Church requires " an immunity from coercive constraint or restraint by any human power in society or State, whether in the exercise of spiritual authority or in the communal living of the Christian life. [34]

Two general areas of freedom are distinguished. The first includes the internal affairs of the community, its organization, manner of rule, worship, religious growth, the selection, training, appoint-

[31] Walter Abbott (ed.), *The Documents of Vatican II* (New York: Guild, America, & Association Presses, 1966), p. 685.

[32] Murray, " The Issue of Church and State at Vatican Council II, " p. 587.

[33] Abbott, *op. cit.*, p. 693.

[34] Murray, " The Issue of Church and State at Vatican Council II, " p. 589.

ment, and transferral of ministers, communications with other churches, the erection of churches and schools, and the possession of property. The second includes the external action of the community, its public witness to its own faith as such, and its further witness to the values of its faith in their relations to the affairs of the temporal order. [35]

The Church therefore requires freedom to fulfill the mandate of Christ to preach His gospel and to observe His commandments. The mandate given the Church is a truth of the transcendent order and not subject to or even accessible to the judgment of the State. At the same time the Church reminds the powers of the secular order to recognize not only her freedom but the freedom of all men, because of their basic human dignity, for both personal and corporate religious life.

What then does the Church ask of governments? What she can ask was magnificently stated by Paul VI on December 8, 1965, in an address to the statesmen of the world:

> And what is it that the Church asks of you, after almost two thousand years of all manner of vicissitudes in her relations with you, the powers of earth—what is it that she asks of you today? In one of the major texts of the Council she has told you what it is. She asks of you nothing but freedom—freedom to believe and to preach her faith, freedom to love God and to serve Him, freedom to live and to bring men her message of life. [36]

The Constitution on the Church in the Modern

[35] Abbott, *op. cit.*, p. 682.
[36] *Acta Apostolicae Sedis*, LVIII (1966), pp. 10-11.

World also faces the question of the Church and the State. The mission of the Church is not of the political, economic, or social order. In consequence, the Church is not bound to any particular form of human culture, or to any political, economic, or social system. In further consequence, her ardent wish is " that, standing in the service of the good of all, she may be able to develop freely under any form of government which recognizes the fundamental rights of the person and of the family, and also recognizes the exigencies of the common good. " [37]

To the transcendence of the Church are linked the universality of her mission and her freedom to accomplish it. However, transcendence to the world does not mean isolation from the world. The Church is to serve as " the leaven, as it were, the soul of human society, which is to be renewed in Christ and transformed into the family of God. " [38] From now on the Church defines her mission in the temporal order in terms of the realization of human dignity, the promotion of the rights of men, the growth of the human family toward unity, and the sanctification of the secular activities of the world. The mission of the Church in the temporal order still remains a spiritual mission.

The Constitution goes on to affirm that the political community and the Church are independent of each other and are autonomous, each in its own field. However, harmony and cooperation are to

[37] Abbott, *op. cit.*, p. 242.
[38] *Ibid.*, p. 239.

exist between the Church and the State, not only because both hold command and rule over the same body of men, the same one man who is at once citizen and Christian, but because each order, " yet by a different title, serves the personal and social vocation of the same human beings. " [39]

Cooperation of the Church and the State in the service of the human person is stated as a principle. The concrete forms of cooperation are to be instituted under regard for circumstances of place and time. Cooperation, both as a matter of principle and in the various forms of its realization, is required by reason of the dual nature of the human person: " For man is not restricted to the temporal sphere. While living in history he fully maintains his eternal vocation. " [40]

From what has been written about the general principles governing the Church and the State as formulated by Gustave Weigel and John Courtney Murray and from the documents of Vatican II, no conflict should arise in Catholic circles about accepting the basic concepts of shared time education. Fundamental to shared time is the principle of cooperation for the service of the human person. The State and the Church cooperate in the education of the child. Both are at the service of the child. At the same time, in the program the Church limits herself to her purely spiritual character, the religious development of the child, the area in which the

[39] *Ibid.*, p. 288.
[40] *Ibid.*

Church is commissioned and best qualified while the State assumes the secular or temporal education, the area in which the State is best qualified. Shared time then is not only in conformity with the mind and spirit of Vatican II and the basic principles governing the Church and the State but the program enables both institutions to fulfill their missions with due regard for the dignity of the child and the right of conscience of the members.

The American tradition

Sharing the education of the individual between the schools of the State and the schools of the Church is not as foreign to the American scene as many may think. Throughout the course of the history of the United States, numerous occasions have arisen when forms of shared time education, although they were not called by this name, were either recommended or actually tried. Unfortunately, the climate of ecumenical dialogue was not what it is in the 1960's and many efforts for cooperation between the Church and the State in education produced little results.

Perhaps the earliest efforts to seek cooperation between Church and State in education were those of Thomas Jefferson. " From the year that Jefferson left the presidential office in 1809 to his death in 1826, two preoccupations seem paramount among his varied interests. " [1] Jefferson sought to show his clerical critics that he was not a devil, infidel or atheist. He urged several of his friends to join him in extracting the " simple, " " unadulterated, " and " genuine " moral teachings of Christ from the " travesties, " " sophistications, " and " artifical

---

[1] Joseph Costanzo, *This Nation Under God* (New York: Herder and Herder, 1964), p. 74.

constructions " which the clergy in their greed for power and wealth grafted to the " pure " teaching of Jesus. Concurrent with this personal consideration, Jefferson's major efforts were involved in the planning of the State educational systems in Virginia. Often the two became inter-twined. Jefferson had a deep conviction of the theological basis of society; for him the complete circle of the useful sciences included sectarian teaching and worship. His educational proposals of 1814, 1817, 1818, 1822, and 1824 manifested his contempt of supernatural creeds which he repeatedly ridiculed; yet despite his dogmatic intolerance, Jefferson held inviolate the equal and impartial protection by law of freedom for all religions in institutions of learning. An individual, because of religion, could neither suffer civil incapacitations nor incur inequality of circumstances and benefits in the schools of the State. [2]

On September 7, 1814, Jefferson wrote a letter to his nephew, Peter Carr, outlining a comprehensive plan of education for Virginia to be supported by State funds. Included in Jefferson's proposals were three types of schools—the elementary, general, and professional. In the professional school there would be a department of « Theology and Ecclesiastical History, » to which the " ecclesiastic " would come as would the lawyer, physician, soldier, etc., come to their own proper studies. [3]

In the initial proposal Jefferson was silent on

[2] Saul K. Padover (ed.), *The Complete Jefferson* (New York: Duell, 1943), pp. 955-56.

[3] *Ibid.*, p. 1067.

the place of religious instruction in the elementary school. He probably felt that the study of theology and ecclesiastical history should be kept for the professional grades since younger children would not be able to cope with surprise indoctrination by teachers of religion other than their own. Jefferson evidently considered this problem during the intervening three years for in the draft of an " Act of Establishing Elementary Schools " which was submitted to the Generaly Assembly of Virginia on September 9, 1817, he wrote that " no religious reading, instruction, or exercise, shall be prescribed or practices inconsistent with the tenets of any religious sect or denomination. " [4] Jefferson strove to protect the religious conscience of the young by proscribing only what was inconsistent with the tenets of any religion.

In 1818, in the formal planning of the curriculum for the University of Virginia, Jefferson abandoned an earlier provision for a department of theology and ecclesiastical history. He explained his change in attitude for sectarian teaching by the State itself in terms of reasons of principle. The State constitution by the Act of 1786 abandoned religious establishment, and thus it would be offensive for the State to provide a professor of a particular sect. At the same time it would be financially impossible to provide professors of divinity for every denomination. It would not be an offense to the constitution, " to leave every sect to provide, as they think fittest,

[4] *Ibid.*, p. 1076.

the means of further instruction in their own particular tenets. " [5]   However, the teaching of the proofs of God and His moral law by the professor of ethics who would appeal not to revealed theology but to the construction of natural theology and ethics on the unitive basis of reason, " in which all sects agree " would be proper and sufficient surrogate. [6]

Faced with numerous misrepresentations, Jefferson in 1822, reexamined the report of 1818 and made clear that a totally non-religious education was a defective one, and he went on to describe the close cooperation that should exist between the University of Virginia and the sectarian religions. A positive plan in favor of religious education was put forth with explicit concern for impartiality. Jefferson established that neutrality, total abstention, was not the only universal, impartial disposition by law to avoid inequities. [7]

Jefferson in the full stature of a great statesman insisted upon the equal rights of all religions before the law, and as an educator he appreciated the scholastic benefits of bringing the various religions together on a university level. He formulated a remedy that was both positive in its provisions in favor of religious studies and guaranteed against a favoritism that encroached on anyone's religious conscience. The various denominations were invited to establish their schools of divinity on State university property. Although the facilities of the

[5] *Ibid.*, p. 1104.
[6] *Ibid.*
[7] *Ibid.*, p. 957.

university were open to the students of these schools, the schools of divinity would be independent of the university and of each other. [8]

In 1824, Thomas Jefferson, now rector of the University of Virginia, drew up the regulations for the university which would actually open its doors in March of 1825. He again reiterated the invitations to religious sects to build on the university grounds. Students would " be free, and expected to attend religious worship at the establishment of their respective sects, in the morning, and in time to meet their school in the university at its stated hour. " [9] If the students of religion needed rooms for religious worship or for lectures and examinations, one of the large eliptical rooms might be used for such purposes. [10]

Jefferson strongly advocated shared cooperation between the State and the Church in education. At first he was silent about the place of religion on the elementary level. Later the silence was broken when he stipulated that religion should be left to the university since he feared that children would be unduly influenced if they received instructions from those of other persuasions. In systems which would provide teachers from their own church, Jefferson might have been more inclined to fulfill the circle of knowledge even on the elementary level. Whatever the case might be, separation of Church and State did not mean for Thomas Jefferson the exclusion of

[8] *Ibid.*, p. 958.
[9] *Ibid.*, p. 1110.
[10] *Ibid.*, p. 1111.

religious education from the school; rather it implied cooperation and that religion should be cared for by the society best suited to undertake the teaching of theology, the Church.

Although Jefferson had fought vigorously for the freedom of religious conscience on all levels of education, his cry went unheeded. Catholics though small in number, at first had supported the common or public schools. By 1849, the public schools took on a marked Protestant hue. The so-called non-sectarian, public schools with their teachers did no violence to Protestant beliefs. Bible reading (from the King James version) with or without instruction, prayer and sacred hymns were part of the non-sectarian religion in the common schools, academies, and colleges. The generally Protestant tone of the public schools could hardly be accepted by Catholics.

To safeguard the religious life of their children, Catholics established parochial schools. Catholics not only had to support these schools but also had to pay their full share of taxes to underwrite the public schools. " Here plainly was a problem of double taxation for education, a condition which came into being with the rise of the public school system. "[11]

In July 1840, John Hughes, Bishop of New York, started a drive for State funds for Catholic schools. William Seward, Governor of New York, had recommended the establishment of religious schools with State funds. Controversy arose over

[11] Daniel F. Reilly, *The Catholic School Controversy* (Washington: Catholic University of America Press, 1943), p. 12.

both the drive and the proposal and non-Catholics
were aligned politically against any State or city aid
to elementary denominational schools. [12]

Refused aid by the City Council and faced with
the rise of the Know-Nothing movement, the
Protestant hue of public schools, and their increased
secularization, the path seemed clear to John
Hughes: the Church must establish and maintain
her own schools and finance them alone. Thus
Hughes declared:

> We must then look forward to the organization of
> schools, and what is more, if they force it upon us, we
> must look forward to the expurgation of books. So that
> if we are ultimately obliged to educate Catholic children
> at the expense of second taxation—that is, when they
> first take our taxes and transfer them to an irresponsible
> corporation that uses them not for our benefit, and only
> return them in the way that injures us, we must have a
> second recourse to our purses—then, indeed, we shall
> study that ours will be thorough education, and a thor-
> ough Catholic education. [13]

Catholics suffered for their stand in education,
and in defense some members condemned public
schools as being per se evil, and Catholic parents who
sent their children to them, even because of exten-
uating circumstances, were criticized. A voice
crying in the wilderness was that of Orestes Brownson who, in July 1859, urged his fellow Catholics
to guard against such a pitfall. This type of thinking

[12] A. K. McClure, *Recollections of Half a Century* (Salem, Mass.,
1902), pp. 216-18.

[13] Lawrence Kehoe (ed.), *Complete Works of the Most Reverend
John Hughes* (New York: Catholic Publication, 1864), p. 249.

would denationalize the American Catholic and tend to keep Catholics a foreign colony in the United States. [14]   Catholics were asked to look upon the good points of the public schools and aid in their improvement and removal of whatever was repugnant to the Catholic conscience.

Brownson's voice was not heard.   Consequently, when the Second Plenary Council of Baltimore met in October 1866, it restated the decrees of the First Plenary Council, which had met in 1852, that schools were to be established in connection with all churches. [15]   Since the Second Plenary Council had not spoken in stronger terms, the matter was carried to the Sacred Congregation *De Propaganda Fide* which issued in 1875, with papal approval, its important " Instruction to the Bishops of the United States Concerning Public Schools. "   The " Instruction " cited the dangers to the faith and morals of children attending public schools.   Attendance at such schools was forbidden and Catholic children could attend only if dangers to faith and morals had been made remote by proper safeguards.   Parents who disregarded their responsibility in this matter could not be absolved. [16]

Some Catholic educators went so far as to consider education strictly a private undertaking,

[14] Orestes Brownson, "Public and Parochial Schools," *Brownson's Quarterly Review*, New York Series, IV (1859), p. 330.

[15] *Conciliorium Provincialium et Plenarii Baltimorensium, Decreta* (Baltimore, 1853), n. 13.

[16] *Acta et Decreta Concilii Plenarii Baltimorensis Tertii* (Baltimore: John Murphy, 1886), Appendix, 279.

independent of the State. Thus, for example, a Jesuit wrote in the *American Catholic Quarterly Review* in 1877: " The only educational taxes that can be reasonably defended are those which go to the support of orphans and helpless children. " [17]

The State then was granted no direct role in education. Its only prerogative was to compel parents to educate their children and to assist them financially. A chief justice of the Supreme Court of Arizona, Edmund F. Dunne, speaking on behalf of a group of Catholics in that State wrote: " We, that is, those for whom I now argue maintain (1) That the State has no right to teach religion; (2) That the State has no right to teach irreligion; (3) That the State has no inherent right to teach at all. " [18]

The zenith in theory was achieved in the ideal formulated by the Third Plenary Council of Baltimore in 1884, which even to this day has been an unfulfilled ideal: " Every Catholic child in a Catholic school. " The Council decreed that near each church which did not have a school, within two years from the promulgation of the Council, schools were to be established, and Catholic parents were bound to send their children to them,

> unless either at home or even in other Catholic schools they may sufficiently and evidently provide for the Christian education of their children, or unless it be

[17] P. Bayma, " The Liberalistic View of the Public School Question, " *American Catholic Quarterly Review*, II (1877), p. 2.

[18] Edmund F. Dunne, *Our Public Schools: Are They Free or Are They Not?* (New York: Thomas Egan, 1875), p. 3.

lawful to send them to other schools on account of a sufficient cause, approved by the bishop and with opportune cautions and remedies.   As to what is a Catholic school, it is left to the judgment of the Ordinary to define. [19]

Although the main stream of Catholic thought was directed toward the view that there would be no cooperation between the Church and the schools of the State, there were a few instances in which the Church and the State actually collaborated in education.   One of the earliest programs was the Lowell Plan in Massachusetts.   At a town meeting of May 3, 1830, through the instigation of the Rev. Theodore Edison, rector of St. Anne's Episcopal Church and lifelong friend of the Irish Catholics, the school committee was authorized for that year only to expend fifty dollars for the education of Irish children in Lowell; " and that committee—making a bold innovation hitherto unparalleled in New England— simply turned over this part of the public funds as a subsidy to the existing Catholic school. " [20]   For the following year, the school board offered a school for the exclusive use of the Irish which was to be supported by public funds and was to be conducted like any other school.   The Irish desired the school should have Catholic teachers, Catholic textbooks, and Catholic religious instruction, none of which the board was willing to grant.   On April 4, 1831, a

[19] *Acta et Decreta Concilii Plenari Baltimorensis Tertii*, pp. 713-18.

[20] Robert H. Lord, John E. Sexton, and Edward T. Harrington, *History of the Archdiocese of Boston*, Vol. II (New York: Sheed and Ward, 1944), p. 314.

town meeting voted establishment of a public school
for Irish children only. " The public school for the
Irish had money but few pupils; the Catholic school,
now lodged in the basement of St. Patrick's church,
had pupils, but little money. " [21]

The unsatisfactory condition lasted for four
years. At the initiative of Rev. Peter Connolly, the
assistant pastor of St. Patrick's, negotiations were
reopened. The school committee entered readily
into Connolly's views and a compromise was reached
which met the approval of both sides. The essence
of the Agreement of 1835 was as follows:

> 1) The Committee consented to adopt and support as
> town schools both the school established in the basement
> of St. Patrick's (June 14th) and, shortly afterwards, one
> which Father Connolly had recently set up in the Chapel
> Hill section (September 14th). 2) These schools were
> to have only Catholic teachers (and in fact the previous
> masters, Patrick Collins and Daniel McIlroy, were
> retained). 3) The books, exercises, and studies should
> all be prescribed and regulated by the Committee, and
> none other whatever should be taught or allowed. But
> no book or regulation should be introduced... derogat-
> ing from, or reflecting upon the character of the Catholic
> religion, directly or indirectly;... and no new textbooks
> dealing with controversial subjects should be adopted
> without the approval of a priest. [22]

According to the regulations issued in 1836 by the
school board, ten minutes daily were devoted to
religious exercises in public schools, and in the
Catholic schools these exercises were to consist of

[21] *Ibid.*, p. 315.
[22] *Ibid.*

prayers and the reading of any book that might be approved by the subcommittee of those schools. [23]

In 1843, however, the system began to break down. One primary requisite for the program's successful operation was the maintenance of constant, close cooperation between the annually elected school committee and the Catholic pastors of Lowell. It would have been ideal if one of the pastors could have served on the school committee, but even in Lowell liberality had not yet advanced to the point where the election of a priest, or of any Catholic, would be considered.

Rev. James McDermott, pastor of St. Patrick's from 1837 to 1847, had difficulty within his own flock. In 1843, McDermott became dissatisfied with a group of Catholic teachers whom he himself had helped to appoint, apparently because of their supposed neglect of their religious duties. Under McDermott's influence parents forwarded petitions to the school committee requesting dismissal of seven out of the nine Catholic teachers. Except for James Egan, principal of the grammar school, the accused teachers refused to resign.

Catholics divided into two factions, those in agreement with McDermott and those opposed. The school committee, finding no specific charges or evidence against the six teachers, refused to discharge them. Father McDermott then ordered the children of his parish to go on strike as long as the six remained. For a few weeks the schools

[23] *Records, Lowell School Committee* (November 8, 1836).

were almost deserted, but the board, the Catholic opposition to McDermott, and the teachers stood firm. The strike failed and in the end McDermott failed.

The unhappy affair marked a turning point. For the first time since the Agreement of 1835, the school committee had opposed the views of the Catholic pastor and had done so with the approval of a large part of the Catholics. Henceforth, contact was completely broken between the Board and the chief Catholic pastor of the city. The school committee was indignant over what had happened and there was serious thought of breaking away from the program. They decided, however, to continue with the program but it would be practiced in a different spirit.

In September 1844, two Protestants were appointed to fill two vacancies in the Irish Grammar School. In December, Martin Flynn, a Catholic, resigned as principal of that school, and was succeeded by George Shattuck, a Protestant. By March 1845, out of twelve teachers in the schools, only six were Catholics. In 1846 the Catholic quota had shrunk to three out of twelve. The schools were still called Irish and their number increased as the Celtic population increased. By 1841 there were eleven such schools: one grammar and ten primaries, with only five Catholics employed that year. Even the principle of separate schools was imperfectly maintained for there were a few Yankee pupils in the Irish schools, and there were Irish children in all the schools of the city.

The Agreement of 1835 had gone by the board. No priest any longer had a voice in the management of the Irish schools. Since 1847 St. Patrick's no longer housed any of them. The curriculum, teaching staff (with few exceptions), and the atmosphere were indistinguishable from the public schools.

> In short, the native Americans of Lowell had attained the purpose for which they entered into the Agreement. They had coaxed the Irish into the public schools. But the Irish in the end had been disappointed in virtually all the hopes which they had based upon that arrangement. It is not surprising, then, that in 1852, when Father John O'Brien brought in the Sisters of Notre Dame to start St. Patrick's parochial school, both sides agreed that the system of 1835 was dead. [24]

Another effort at cooperation was the Poughkeepsie plan. In 1873 the Rev. Patrick McSweeney, pastor of St. Peter's church, Poughkeepsie, New York, developed a program with the local school board whereby the parochial school was rented for one dollar a year, and its furnishings and maintenance were undertaken by the board. The teachers, which included the Sisters of Charity, were selected, paid, and subject to dismissal by the board; there was tacit agreement not to hire teachers other than Catholics, as long as they were competent. Textbooks other than history, reading, and geography were selected by the board. Religion was given after the regular school hours, and no child was

[24] Lord, *op. cit.*, p. 319.

required to attend religious instructions without the consent of the parents. [25]

The Jesuits were the first patrons of a program like Poughkeepsie's. According to Archbishop John Ireland the Jesuits had developed such programs in Florissant, Missouri, and in Conewago, Pennsylvania. [26] Catholics had made arrangements with school authorities, which incorporated in them the main features of the plan in Connecticut, Georgia, Pennsylvania, New Jersey, and New York. [27]

The Church in the United States was dividing into two camps, those who opposed the schools of the State and those who favored cooperation in various degrees. It was no wonder then that the address of Archbishop John Ireland to the National Educational Association at St. Paul, Minnesota, in July, 1890, hit the American Church with a blast which was sounded from coast to coast and around the world. Without a doubt no other speech like it on Catholic and State schools had ever before been uttered in the United States by an archbishop.

The address was entitled " State Schools and Parish Schools. " Ireland was mainly concerned with the possibility of union between the two educational systems. In the first part he considered the State school and openly granted the right of the State to

[25] John A. Burns and Bernard J. Kohlbrenner, *A History of Catholic Education in the United States* (New York: Benziger, 1937), p. 160.

[26] John Ireland, *The Church and Modern Society* (Chicago, 1897), I, p. 212.

[27] Reilly, *op. cit.*, p. 76.

establish schools and to require compulsory attendance of all children at some school. Ireland stated
that he was not only a friend but an advocate of the
State school. Conditions of the time made Ireland
uphold the parish school, though he sincerely desired
that they should not have to exist. The parish
schools were necessary since the State schools ten-
ded to eliminate religion from the minds and hearts
of the children. Teaching of morals would not be
sufficient. Catholics demanded religion and, therefore, had to have their own schools. The Archbishop
said, " I express my regret that there is a necessity
for its existence. In behalf of the State school I call
upon my fellow Americans to aid in the removal
of the necessity. " [28]

Ireland then considered the burden of double
taxation for education endured by Catholics. He
offered two tentative solutions: first, he

> would permeate the regular State school with the
> religion of the majority of the children of the land, be
> this religion as Protestant as Protestantism can be, and
> would, as is done in England, pay for the secular instruc-
> tion given in denominational schools according to
> results, that is, every pupil passing the examination before
> State officials, and in full accordance with the State
> program, would secure to his school the cost of the
> tuition of a pupil in the State school. This is not paying
> for religious instruction, but for the secular instruction
> demanded by the State, and given to the pupil as thor-
> oughly as he could have received it in the State school. [29]

[28] Ireland, *op. cit.*, p. 202.
[29] *Ibid.*, p. 211.

The second plan Ireland offered was the Pough-keepsie program which was used in New York and in other places in the United States. Ireland ended his talk by saying that Catholics demanded the Christian state school. [30]

With the approval of John Ireland, between August and October, 1891, two pastors of the Archdiocese of St. Paul, Rev. James Conry of Immaculate Conception Church at Fairbault, Minnesota, and Rev. Charles Corcoran of St. Michael Church in Stillwater, entered into agreements with their respective school boards to rent their parish schools for one dollar a year with stipulations similar to those which had been developed in Poughkeepsie. When the details became known, the smoldering effects of Ireland's education address were rekindled; there was an immediate cry from some Catholics who accused him of abandoning the Catholic school system, while many non-Catholics charged him with trying to take over the public schools from within. The lines of battle were drawn; the stage was set; the school controversy had begun.

In itself the school controversy of 1891-1903 was perhaps one of the most interesting periods in the history of the American Catholic Church. The details and personalities were most extensive; however, the man who shines forth the brightest was Thomas Joseph Bouquillon.

Thomas Bouquillon was born at Warneton, Belgium on May 16, 1840. His education took

[30] *Ibid.*

place at the local schools and at the College of St. Louis in Menin, Belgium. In 1862, he entered the seminary at Bruges; his talents were noted by his superiors who directed him to continue in Rome at the Capranica College where he was ordained in 1867 after receiving a Doctorate in Sacred Theology from the Gregorian University. In 1869, Bouquillon was appointed professor of moral theology at the seminary of Bruges. After ten years of teaching at Bruges, he was named professor of moral theology at the University of Lille in France. Bouquillon was forced by ill health to leave Lille, and in retreat and retirement devoted four years to research at the Benedictine Monastery of Maredsous in Belgium.

It was during this time that Bishop John Keane, the first rector of the Catholic University of America, was traveling through Europe in search of a faculty for the university. Keane was attracted to Bouquillon because of the reception given to the publication of his manual on moral theology, *Theologia Moralis Fundamentalis*.

Bouquillon occupied the chair of moral theology at the Catholic University of America until his death on November 5, 1902. He served as confidant to two rectors, Bishops John J. Keane and Thomas J. Conaty, and held for a time the position of Dean of the School of Theology. His *Theologia Moralis Fundamentalis* went to three editions. From his pen flowed more than fifty articles—critical, theological, historical.

Bouquillon's most famous work appeared in November of 1891, a thirty-one page brochure

entitled, *Education: To Whom Does It Belong?* To
understand properly the background for the reception which this work received, it is necessary to
know something of the internal conflicts which the
Catholic Church in the United States and especially
at the Catholic University were involved in at the
time. When the University was formerly opened
on November 13, 1889, the hierarchy of the United
States was divided into opposite camps. Each group
felt that his attitude on divisive issues was the more
orthodox and, therefore, to be maintained at all
costs. One group was called by the secular press
of the time the liberal or progressive party with
John Ireland its recognized leader. The other group
was called the ultramontane, or conservative party,
with Michael A. Corrigan, Archbishop of New York,
directing its destinies. During its early years Catholic University suffered, not because any single
bishop was opposed to it, as such, but because the
first rector, John J. Keane, was so strikingly iden-
tified with the liberals. As a result the university
project naturally received its greatest support from
that wing of the hierarchy and it suffered its
principal opposition at the hands of the so-called
conservatives.

   In 1891, the famous school controversy broke
over the Church of the United States. The controversy rallied the opposing groups to their post
once more. " Corrigan, McQuaid (Bishop of Rochester), and the German-American bishops hit at the
Fairbault-Stillwater plan of John Ireland, aided as
they were by several Jesuit writers, and by

Monsignor Joseph Schroeder, professor of dogmatic theology at the Catholic University of America. " [31] The faculty of the Catholic University was divided on the matter with Keane and Bouquillon taking sides with Ireland while Schroeder gave his support to the German Catholics and the Jesuits who were opposed to the Ireland position. Cardinal Gibbons' sympathies were clearly with Ireland, yet as chancellor of the Catholic University he tried to moderate the feelings of both parties. [32]

Although *Education: To Whom Does It Belong?* consisted of only thirty-one pages, the work had a thunderous impact upon the life of the Church in the United States. Some felt that Bouquillon, as a foreigner, was nothing more than a meddler. Others looked upon the work as an effort to give doctrinal basis for Ireland's Fairbault-Stillwater plan. The truth of the matter was that the work was the result of Bouquillon's ordinary class lectures and two addresses which he delivered at St. Mary's Seminary in Baltimore. Cardinal Gibbons, when he had read the text, urged its publication in the *Catholic Quarterly*.

What did Bouquillon's pamphlet contain? In his preface the author stated the *raison d'être* of the work. The pamphlet was written at the request of his ecclesiastical superiors and dealt with only theo-

---

[31] Peter E. Hogan, *The Catholic University of America, 1896-1903—The Rectorship of Thomas J. Conaty* (Washington: Catholic University of America Press, 1949), p. 142.

[32] John Tracy Ellis, *The Life of James Cardinal Gibbons* Milwaukee: Bruce, 1952), p. 425.

retical principles. The superiors of Bouquillon felt that the air of controversy stimulated by the school question should be cleared so that the exposition of principles would be helpful and useful at this time.

Bouquillon made no pretense to originality but stated frankly that he walked in the footsteps of the great theologians, especially of Thomas Aquinas, and he was guided by the writings of Leo XIII. In order to complete his treatment Bouquillon felt that it would be necessary for him to treat certain delicate points on which even Catholics were not in agreement. [33]

In the introduction which followed the preface Bouquillon stated in outline exactly what he would treat in the study. It was to consist of four questions: the right to educate, the mission to educate, authority over education, and the liberty of education. These were to be considered in view of the individual, the family, the State, and the Church. In facts, principles, and laws, he looked for answers to the questions under discussion.

Bouquillon searched for the exposition of principles in the more recent writers rather than in the older ones who lived before the era of separation of Church and State. He was especially influenced by Suarez, Leo XIII, and Cardinal Newman; those whose views were contrary to his own were also quoted. Bouquillon stated his main sources and explained what principles guided him in the writing of the pamphlet.

[33] Thomas Bouquillon, *Education: To Whom Does It Belong?* (Baltimore: John Murphy, 1891), p. 4.

Before treating the right of the State to educate,
Bouquillon defined what he meant by the terms
" right " and " person. "   A " right . . . is a faculty,
moral and inviolable, of doing, exacting, possessing,
and disposing of something, " while only a " ra-
tional being is capable of possessing a right; such
a being, as possessing a right, is properly called
a person; if one who possesses the right is a corporation, a college, the person is moral. " [34]

" The parents are entitled (by God) to be the
first instructors of their children themselves, or
through teachers of their own choosing. " [35]   The
right of parents was extensive but not unlimited or
independent.   Referring to Leo XIII, Bouquillon
stated that a father did not have the right to deprive
his child of religious instructions.   It was then the
duty of parents to give their children an education
which would make them both good citizens and
good Christians.

Parents could not, ordinarily, lose their right
to educate.   If the State established public schools,
it was bound to take account of the reasonable
wishes of parents and allow them a legitimate share
in the carrying on of such schools.   Primary schools
were not to be governmental, as in some countries,
but municipal as in the United States, since the
municipality more nearly and completely represented
the families and was the immediate emanation of
them.

For Bouquillon the Church, too, was a teaching

[34] *Ibid.*, p. 7.
[35] *Ibid.*, p. 10.

power. The Church's duty was to make known to man his relations to God, his end; the rules which should be followed and the means which he should use to attain that end. The Church by its divine constitution had direct authority over religious instruction and indirect authority over secular instruction.

> But the Church has not received the mission to make known the human sciences, she has not been established for the progress of nations in the arts and sciences.... Doubtless, in virtue of the general harmony that reigns between all things, the Church, while communicating the science of things heavenly, contributes powerfully to the development of human sciences; just as she contributes to the temporal happiness and strength of nations by inculcating the practice of the supernatural virtues. But this is a result and not the object proper of the mission of the Church. Her duty of teaching human sciences is only indirect, a work of charity or of necessity; of charity when they are not sufficiently taught by others who have that duty; of necessity, when they are badly taught, that is, taught in a sense opposed to supernatural truth and morality. [36]

According to Bouquillon the State had a special and proper right to educate but this right was not absolute since the State could not teach error; the right was not exclusive since the State might not hinder others, notably the family and the Church from teaching, and the exercise of this right was subject to the moral law which governed States and individuals. [37]

[36] *Ibid.*, p. 20.
[37] *Ibid.*, p. 12.

The demonstration of the State's right to educate was formulated in the following syllogism:

> Civil authority has the right to use all the legitimate temporal means it judges necessary for the attainment of the temporal common welfare. Now, among the most necessary means for the attainment of the temporal welfare of the commonwealth, is the diffusion of human knoweldge. Therefore, civil authority has the right to use the means necessary for the diffusion of such knowledge, that is to say, to teach it, or rather to have it taught by capable agents. [38]

After religious instruction, civil instruction was the first means of civilizing a people. The State was bound to provide scientific, technical, and industrial training to safeguard its members against fraud and injustice, so that the members of the State could know persons and things, and know the laws which regulated relations between the persons, the enjoyment and use of things, and the exercise of rights. The teaching power of the State then meant the establishing of schools, the appointing of teachers, the prescribing of methods and programs of study. This was accomplished in the same way as the State governed and judged, that is, through delegates fitted for such function. The right then of the State to teach profane sciences was essentially within its natural domain. [39]

The State then had the mission of providing education in the letters, sciences, and arts. This duty was comprised in the general duty of providing for

[38] *Ibid.*
[39] *Ibid.*, p. 12.

the common good. The mission came from God, when God created man a social being, just as parents received their mission to be the educators of their children, when God granted them children. The mission of the State to educate was an accidental function, supplying the insufficieny of individuals. The State need not exercise its mission in all circumstances but could and should exercise it only when necessity or utility demanded the State's intervention. " Individuals, families, associations, may have provided all the education that is necessary. In that case the State is freed from its obligation. " [40]

The authority of the State to educate was not absolute, nor arbitrary, nor exclusive of the Church and the family. In the divine plan these three authorities should combine their efforts for the common good. The authority of the State was included in that general authority with which the State was invested for promoting the common good. From this came the authority of the State to make education compulsory and to demand a minimum of instruction. [41]

In his closing paragraph, Bouquillon gave answer in summary form to the question which was the title of his work:

> Education: To whom does it belong? This is the question with which we started out. We now make answer. It belongs to the individual, physical or moral, to the family, to the State, to the Church, to none of these solely and exclusively, but to all four combined in harmonious

[40] *Ibid.*, p. 19.
[41] *Ibid.*, pp. 22-28.

working for the reason that man is not an isolated but a social being. Precisely in the harmonious combination of these four factors in education is the difficulty of practical application. Practical application is the work of the men whom God has placed at the head of the Church and the State, not ours. [42]

The first to launch an attack upon Bouquillon was René I. Holaind, S.J., a former professor of ethics in the Jesuit scholasticate at Woodstock, Maryland. Holaind listed six main objections to Bouquillon's work, the essence of which were that the moralist had granted too much authority to the State in education. [43]

In 1892, Bouquillon prepared and published a second pamphlet entitled, *Education: To Whom Does It Belong? A Rejoinder to Critics*. In it he took issue with Holaind and answered him point by point.

Bishops took sides against bishops; theologians against theologians, and even Jesuits against Jesuits. Catholic journals and newspapers fought against each other. The controversy reached Rome and in the January 2, 1892 issue of the *Civiltà Cattolica*, a review of importance published by the Jesuits, Salvatore M. Brandi, one of the editors, severely criticized Bouquillon. Brandi felt that the moralist had granted to the State rights which did not belong to it. He attacked Bouquillon's position on compulsory education, writing that although compulsory

[42] *Ibid.*, p. 31.
[43] R. Holaind, *The Parent First: An Answer to Dr. Bouquillon's Query, ' Education: To Whom Does It Belong? '* (New York: Benziger Brothers, 1892).

education was necessary to civil society, it did not follow that it had to be under the dominion of the State. Bouquillon's use of Leo XIII and Aquinas were considered as *non ad rem.* [44]

Such criticism in the *Civiltà Cattolica* called for a separate answer by Bouquillon, a forty-one page rejoinder. It was a masterpiece of controversial writing and answered every point raised in the Roman review.

During this time Archbishop Ireland traveled to Rome striving to obtain approval of this Fairbault-Stillwater arrangement, and thereby obtaining approval for the notions of Bouquillon. On April 21, 1892, the Congregation of the Propaganda with the approval of Leo XIII issued the now famous *Tolerari Potest* decree, which stated in part that although the sound decrees of the Baltimore Council remained fully in force, the agreement made by Ireland with regard to the Fairbault and Stillwater schools, all the circumstances being taken into consideration, could be allowed (*tolerari potest*). [45]

Although *Tolerari Potest* was neither a condemnation nor a vindication of Bouquillon, it would seem from his reception by Leo XIII that he did not lose the favor he enjoyed with Rome before the controversy began. In August 1893, Leo XIII received Bouquillon in private audience twice, and later in the same month Leo publicly praised Bouquillon for his wisdom and enlightened spirit.

[44] Reilly, *op. cit.*, p. 125.
[45] *Ibid.*, p. 133.

His wisdom and enlightened spirit was to follow the method of the Church, of adapting ecclesiastical traditions to the historical milieu. He considered the conditions of the time, and while writing, had in view the needs of the times, which required that the family, the Church, and the State concur in education. To give each of these its proper due was the intention of Bouquillon, and in order to do so, he had to speak the language of the times without sacrificing one iota of the divine deposit of the Church.

Faced with the decrees of the Third Council of Baltimore and *Tolerari Potest*, Catholics strove to fulfill the ideal of every Catholic child in a Catholic school. As the years rolled by, the Catholic population increased, and the cost of education became more extensive. Gone from the first Sunday sermon in September was the topic of sending children to a Catholic school; now the topic was sending children to religious instruction. Bishops and pastors were faced with a conflict—how to meet the education needs of their children. It was no surprise then that in the spirit of Jefferson and Bouquillon, some turned to shared time education as an answer.

The family, the Church, the State

" The rights and duties of the family, of the Church and of the State as regards education, can never be stressed too much, nor can the mission of each of these three societies with their attributes and proper field of activity, be brought out too clearly. "[1] These words written in a letter from the Vatican Secretariate of State to the IVth Portuguese Social Week, on October 16, 1952, at the direction and with the best wishes of Pius XII, could well have served as the expressed rationale of shared time education. For in shared time, the family, the Church, and the State, the three agencies of education, each with a mission to educate, and with rights and duties, are brought into immediate contact, and are properly ordered to ensure balance and harmony within the total educational process.

The Catholic view of education places man against the backdrop of the total society in which he lives and develops. The means whereby the individual arrives at adult perfection in society is education. " Since education is as extensive as human life itself, different agencies in society share rights and respon-

[1] *Papal Teachings on Education*, edited by the Benedictine Monks of Solesmes, trans. by Aldo Rebeschini (Boston: Daughters of St. Paul, 1960), p. 441.

sibilities in this broad field. " [2]   Man is born into and lives within three societies of the large society: the family, civil society (including the State), and the Church, each with distinct rights to educate.

In expressing the rights of the three agencies of education, philosophers of education with a Catholic orientation have turned to the encyclical *Divini Illius Magistri*, the Christian Education of Youth, by Pius XI issued on December 31, 1929. In its initial effort, the encyclical was a summary on the part of the Pope of the educational thoughts of Pius VII, Leo XII, Gregory XVI, Pius IX, Leo XIII, St. Pius X, and Benedict XV. The work was written against the background of the Roman Question with its settlement in 1929 by the Lateran Treaty; the reign of Mussolini in Italy; excessive statism in France; the seeding of National Socialism in Germany, and of course, the Bolshevik Revolution in Russia and the subsequent rise of Communism; and in general the forced retreat of the Church from the temporal sphere.

For most Catholic philosophers of education the encyclical has served as a landmark instead of a beacon. Consequently, when reviewing the agencies of education, the encyclical has been quoted extensively and without deviation. Dubay in his study of the *Philosophy of the State as Educator*, [3] has relied heavily on the encyclical as have Redden and

[2] Neil G. McCluskey, *Catholic Viewpoint on Education* (Garden City, New York: Doubleday, 1949), p. 80.

[3] Thomas Dubay, *Philosophy of the State as Educator* (Milwaukee: Bruce, 1949), pp. 55-80.

Ryan in *A Catholic Philosophy of Education*,[4] and McCluskey in his *Catholic Viewpoint on Education*.[5]

In his encyclical on Christian education Pius XI teaches that the family into which the child is born has the primary right and obligation to educate. The right is prior to the rights of civil and ecclesiastical society because it is based on the natural relation of parents to their offspring, which is most basic in nature. Because the parents' right to educate flows from the very nature of all concerned, it is an inalienable right. Parents may delegate some of the actual teaching to private and public institutions, but they can in no wise divest themselves of the responsibility for their children's proper formation.

The statist argument that the child is born first a citizen and then an individual is unacceptable. Pius XI forcefully states that " before being a citizen, a man must exist; and existence does not come from the State, but from the parents. "[6]

Although the family's rights in education are basic and inalienable, they are not despotic and absolute. The rights of parents are " necessarily subordinated to the last end and to natural and divine law.[7] Parents then may not send their children to those schools in which there is the danger of " imbibing the deadly poison of impiety. "[8] The obligation to

[4] John Redden and Francis Ryan, *A Catholic Philosophy of Education* (Milwaukee: Bruce, 1956), pp. 344-58.

[5] Neil G. McCluskey, *op. cit.*, pp. 73-96.

[6] *Papal Teachings on Education*, p. 214.

[7] *Ibid.*

[8] *Ibid.*, p. 215.

educate includes not only religious and moral education, but physical and civic education, insofar as it touches upon religion and morality. [9]

In commenting upon Pius XI, Dubay notes that the rights of parents may be conditioned in specific cases by any legitimate authority, civil or ecclesiastical. Catholic parents, therefore, may not send their children to schools precluded by duly established ecclesiastical authority any more than they may reject a just disposition of a duly established civil authority. The State can forbid parents, without depriving them of their freedom or their rights, to send their children to schools which would foster hatred or disloyalty to their country, and the Church can forbid parents in the same way to send their children to schools that will undermine their faith. [10]

According to Pius XI education " belongs preeminently to the Church, by reason of a double title in the supernatural order, conferred exclusively upon it by God Himself; absolutely superior therefore to any other title in the natural order. " [11] The first title is founded upon the direct commission given to the Church by Christ to teach all men: " Go, therefore, and make disciples of all nations... teaching them to observe all that I have commanded you..., " [12] while the second title is that " of supernatural motherhood, in virtue of which the Church,

[9] *Ibid.*
[10] Dubay, *op. cit.*, p. 60.
[11] *Papal Teachings on Education*, p. 205.
[12] Mt 28:19-20.

spotless spouse of Christ, generates, nurtures, and educates souls in the divine life of grace, through her sacraments and her doctrine. " [13]

Whether men recognize the fact or not, the Church has the divinely given duty to lead men to their last end and because of this several derivative rights accrue to the Church. In the exercise of its teaching mission, the Church is independent of any earthly power. The Church may make use of any means that are necessary and useful in the attainment of its end and therefore, " is fully entitled to promote letters, science, and art insofar as is necessary or helpful to Christian education, in addition to its work for the salvation of souls; founding and maintaining schools and institutions adapted to every branch of learning and degree of culture. " [14]

It is the inalienable right, as well as the indispensable obligation of the Church to guard the entire education of its children, in all institutions, whether they are public or private, not merely in regard to religious instructions, " but in regard to every other branch of learning and every regulation insofar as religion and morality are concerned. " [15] This right does not grant the Church the power to interfere with the State's administration of its public schools. [16] It merely protects a field in which the Church alone is competent, the field of religion and morals.

[13] *Papal Teachings on Education*, p. 206.
[14] *Ibid.*, p. 208.
[15] *Ibid.*, pp. 208-9.
[16] *Ibid.*

In viewing the role of the State to educate, Pius XI maintains that although there is a priority of rights on the part of the Church and the family in the field of education, this in no way departs from the " true and just rights of the State in regard to the education of its citizens. "[17]   The rights of the State to educate come from God Himself, in virtue of the authority which it possesses to promote the common temporal welfare.   Education does not belong to the State in the same way as it does to the family and the Church, but in a way corresponding to its own particular end and object.[18]   The State cares for the common temporal welfare through two general functions: protective and promotive.   It must enable the citizen to obtain his temporal and eternal end by warding off unjust interference with the fullfillment of his duties.   This is a protective function.   In a positive way the State must also help the citizen to do what he cannot do for himself and this is a promotive function.

The role of the State in education is founded on both its protective and on its promotive function. As Pius XI states: " The function therefore of the civil authority residing in the State is twofold, to protect and to foster, but by no means to absorb the family and the individual, or to substitute itself for them. "[19]

As far as the protective function of the State is

[17] *Papal Teachings on Education*, p. 217.
[18] *Ibid.*
[19] *Papal Teachings on Education*, p. 218.

concerned, it is the mission of the State to protect the prior rights of the family as well as to respect the supernatural rights of the Church in education. It is also incumbent on the State to protect the rights of the child when the parents are found wanting, " either physically or morally in this respect, whether by default, incapacity or misconduct. " [20] Since the family does not have of itself all the means necessary for its full development, the State in exceptional cases may make provisions for its deficiencies, but in no way does it take the place of the family. [21]

In writing about the promotive educational function of the State, Pius XI teaches that the State should begin " by encouraging and assisting, of its own accord, the initiative and activity of the Church and the family. " [22] The State then should supplement the work of the Church and the family whenever this falls short of what is necessary, even by means of its own schools and institutions. This implies the founding of State schools, when they are needed.

An additional promotive function of the State is the right and duty to exact a minimum amount of education from the generality of its citizens. " The State can exact, and take measure to secure that all its citizens have the necessary knowledge of their civic and political duties, and a certain degree of physical, intellectual, and moral culture, which, considering the conditions of the times, is really

[20] *Ibid.*
[21] *Ibid.*
[22] *Ibid.*, p. 210.

necessary for the common good. " [23]   It would be difficult to determine the amount of knowledge that each citizen should acquire to secure the common good, but the State may exact a minimum educational standard for its citizens.

The State engages in the work of education through the maintenance of institutions necessary for the training of its own personnel. Besides the academies and training programs established for the benefit of the armed forces, under this category would fall those educational enterprises that equip candidates for employment in the various and sundry governmental offices and services.

Finally, Pius XI grants the State in promotive education the right to provide what may be called civic education, not only for youth but for all ages and classes. " This consists in the practice of presenting publicly to groups of individuals information with an intellectual, imaginative and emotional appeal, calculated to draw them toward what is upright and honest, and to urge its practice by a sort of moral compulsion, in the positive sense by disseminating such knowledge, and in the negative sense by suppressing what is opposed to it. " [24]

Aimed as it is at all ages and classes and by no means confined to the school environment, this type of activity on the part of the State might be considered a program of informal education. Under such activities would be included bulletins and lectures dealing with soil conservation, youth problems,

[23] *Papal Teachings on Education,* p. 219.
[24] *Ibid.,* p. 221.

political rights, social security, home building, the erection of air-raid shelters, etc.

Pius XI is very definite in stating that harmony should exist between the Church and the State in education. The fundamental reason for this harmony is that the supernatural order, to which the Church owes her rights, not only does not in the least " destroy the natural order... but elevates that order and perfects it, each affording mutual aid to the other, and completing it in a manner proportional to its respective nature and dignity. " [25] All the orders come from God, and God cannot contradict Himself. Education then is one of those matters that belongs both to the Church and the State, though in different ways. [26]

Thomas Dubay in commenting upon the writings of Pius XI grants the State a genuine role in education, but as a subsidiary educator. Based upon the principle of subsidiarity, from a positive point of view, the government should do for its citizens whatever the latter cannot do for itself. Negatively, it implies that the State should not do what can be done by private initiative. " Subsidiarity, therefore, means that the State is to enter the field of education only when that entrance is necessary or at least beneficial to the common welfare. " [27] The State's function is essentially a supplementary one, that is, the State supplements the work of the primary educators, the Church and the family, whenever and

[25] *Ibid.*, pp. 211-2.
[26] *Ibid.*, p. 222.
[27] Dubay, *op. cit.*, p. 70.

wherever they are unable adequately to carry out a total role in education.

Dubay then sets up an elaborate list of statements to illustrate the reasoning behind his application of a subsidiary role to the State. In part, a total commitment by the State in education runs contrary to the rationale of the State which is to merely supplement what citizens cannot do for themselves. If citizens depend upon the State for education, when they can partake of it themselves through private means, their development, initiative, and freedom will be unreasonably curtailed. The work of education itself suffers from unnecessary State interference and activity. If the State assumes a greater role in education than necessity or utility requires, competition with other educational institutions is either weakened or totally destroyed. Finally a neglect of the principle of subsidiarity in education leads to a loss of freedom for the citizens and can easily result in an intrusion into the rights of conscience since parents may be forced by economic pressures to patronize a school which they do not approve. [28]

For Dubay, then, the State is by nature a protector and promoter of the common welfare. The State therefore is not by nature an educator. The Church and the family on the other hand are by nature educators; such is their very *raison d'être*. " The State's right to educate is indirect: if the common good requires intervention, then the State

[28] *Ibid.*, pp. 70-72.

may and must educate. " [29]   The State directly is bound to care for the general welfare and only for this reason does it enter any field. The educational duty of the Church and the family, on the other hand, does not spring from any inadequacy but is native and direct. The State then teaches not in its own name but in the name and as the delegate of another. " That other can be of course no one but an agency with a direct, underived, primary duty to educate: either the Church or the family. " [30]

This has been the common opinion of Catholic authorities. However, with the renewal taking place in the Church resulting from Vatican II, a new dimension has appeared in the " Catholic " attitude in regard to the agencies of education. The first point of interest is in regard to the Council document on education. The original educational schema was entitled " On Catholic Schools, " but was dropped in favor of the present title " On Christian Education. " Several Fathers of the Council remarked that the Church's educational mission could not be circumscribed by academic education alone. Much of Christian education is given outside of the schools, for example, in the family. At the same time many Fathers felt that a great majority of Catholic young people attend State schools, which have absolutely nothing to do with the Church, when indeed they were not hostile to it.

The Declaration on Christian Education, in itself, is not one of the better documents of the

[29] *Ibid.*, p. 76.
[30] *Ibid.*, p. 77.

Council.   Many Fathers of the Council felt that the document in its final form was too timid, too weak, and too unrealistic, especially with regard to the rights of parents and the competence of the State. Many thought that the rights of parents had been exaggerated and those of the State unduly restricted. The State, it was pointed out, had a much greater part to play in education today.   The State had to assure a much higher standard, it was responsible for providing an equal opportunity for all, and it had to ensure the formation of leaders to administrate the government.   The text as passed by the Council takes a somewhat too simple view of these matters. It emphasizes more strongly than the preliminary drafts the right of parents to choose freely their children's schools and the obligation of the State to make such a free choice possible.   But it reduces the function of the State to providing funds and coordinating the educational system.

The document speaks of the inalienable rights of parents to entrust their children to schools selected by their own choice.   " Consequently, public authority, which has the obligation to oversee and defend the liberties of citizens, ought to see to it, out of a concern for distributive justice, that public subsidies are allocated in such a way that when selecting schools for their children, parents are genuinely free to follow their conscience. " [31]

It is incumbent upon the State to provide citizens with the opportunity to acquire an appro-

[31] Walter Abbott (ed.), *The Documents of Vatican II* (New York: Guild, America & Association Presses, 1966), p. 644.

priate degree of cultural enrichment, and with the proper preparation for exercising their civic duties and rights. The State itself should protect the right of children to receive an adequate schooling. It should be vigilant about the ability of teachers and the excellence of their training. It should look after the health of students and, in general, promote the whole school enterprise. However, there must be no school monopoly. " For such a monopoly would militate against the native rights of the human person, the development and spread of culture itself, the peaceful association of citizens, and the pluralism which exists today in very many societies. " [32]

Three significant interventions were delivered at the third session of Vatican II which indicated the mind of some of the Fathers of the Council on the matter of education. On November 17, 1965, the late John Cardinal Ritter of St. Louis spoke to the Council. He highly praised the proposed schema on education and concurred with the plan that the statement could not be formulated in detail because of the diverse cultures, countries, standards of living, and legal status which the schools and the Church have.

Ritter gave an endorsement to the declaration's affirmation of the freedom of parents to choose the schools they wish for their children. Freedom extends not only to the choice of schools but to the schools themselves. Within their own walls the Catholic schools must be models of Christian freedom in their administration, their teaching, and

[32] *Ibid.*

particularly in the interpersonal relationships among teachers, pupils, and parents. Catholic schools and colleges and universities should not only be free from unjust external coaction and coercion but must be themselves models of Christian freedom.

In conclusion, Cardinal Ritter asked the Fathers to emphasize that Catholic schools do not exist to serve narrow sectarian purposes, nor to protect the selfish interest of the Church. Catholic schools stand as an expression of the free choice and sacrifice of parents, priests, religious, and laity. Catholic schools indeed are and of their very nature must be of substantial benefit to the entire community where they serve and to society itself. If this were not true, Catholic schools would be self-condemned and unworthy of the title Catholic. [33]

On November 18, 1965, Bishop James William Malone, administrator of Youngstown, Ohio called for the Council to probe in depth the agents with rights in education: Church, State, family, private associations, school teachers, administrators, and the students themselves. Bishop Malone requested a further development of the encyclical on education of Pius XI.

The school is not simply the extension of the home or family, and teachers are not simply delegates of the parents or even the Church. Neither is the school simply the agent, much less the servant of

[33] Floyd Anderson (ed.), *Council Daybook Vatican II Session* 3 (Washington, D.C.: National Catholic Welfare Conference, 1965), p. 276.

the State. Each agent in education has a proper
and legitimate interest in the education of its children, but each from its own point of view and within
the limits of its own competence.

In the field of education, the government is not
the official teacher and arbiter of religion, science,
art, literature, music or culture. The State rather
is the servant of the expressed will and consent of
the people " with the right to require that all citizens
are equipped to fulfill their obligations as citizens
within the area of its proper competence. " [34]

Bishop Malone requested that the final schema
repudiate all monopoly in education as an offense
against the dignity of a parent to choose the school
he wishes for his children. The theory of State
monopoly in education is based upon the total
identification of society and the State. " We cannot
answer that monopoly with a theory of family
monopoly, or Church monopoly, in the 20th century. " [35]

The third intervention on the schema of
education which had significance in relation to the
agents of education came from Bishop Hugh
A. Donohue of Stockton, California. Donohue
restated the primary and inalienable right of parents
to choose the schools they wish for their sons and
daughters. " Furthermore, since parents are citizens, they are entitled to equal and equitable
treatment in this choice of schools under the laws of

[34] *Ibid.*, p. 282.
[35] *Ibid.*

their country and do not at all forfeit their right by reason of the religion they profess or the type of school they choose for their children. " [36]   As the State must, the Church too stands willing to help parents fulfill their obligations in education. [37]

In its effort to assist the family, the Church must not forget the schools themselves. It is not sufficient to label a school, its administration, and teaching staff, Catholic. " It is equally necessary that the mark of excellence be the goal and first purpose of the school, its administration and teaching staff. " [38]   The Church should not be mesmerized by mere numbers, but should strive to conduct schools of superior character and excellence. " Achievement is not necessarily proved by statistics. " [39]   At the same time Catholic schools are not defensive weapons existing to shelter and protect children from the world. Rather these schools serve the family and children in preparing students to take their rightful place in the world as witnesses to Christ " not only without fear and with confidence but as well with intelligence and knowledge. " [40]

Bishop Donohue then turned to John XXIII's *Pacem in Terris* where the Holy Father noted that often there is an inconsistency between religious

[36] Intervention of Bishop Hugh A. Donohue of Stockton, California, on the " *Declaratio De Educatione Christiana,* " 1965 (mineographed), p. 1.

[37] *Ibid.*

[38] *Ibid.*

[39] *Ibid.*

[40] *Ibid.*

faith in believers and their activity in the temporal sphere, due in part to a lack of solid Christian education. Too often there is no proportion between scientific training and religious instruction. It is clear that when the Church undertakes to conduct schools, it does so with a dedication to excellence in all branches in learning and not merely in religion, and " when it undertakes the religious education of those not in Church schools, it does so with the same dedication in excellence. " [41]

Turning to the schema's statement that Catholic schools are a true apostotlate, Donohue requested the Council to expand this idea to include all schools whether conducted by the Church, or the State, or by private associations. The apostolate is not only for priests and religious but for the laity as well, most especially those who are teachers in public schools. " Most of the Catholic children and students in the world are in State schools and must be the object of this true apostolate, especially by their teachers. " [42]

If the Church accepts parental rights in education, then Catholic schools must be prepared to accept the role of parents in the determination of policy in the Catholic schools. Laymen are to be accepted not only as teachers but indeed as administrators and presidents of Catholic institutions of learning. [43]

In protecting the rights of parents, the rights of other agents of education are not to be neglected.

[41] *Ibid.*
[42] *Ibid.*
[43] *Ibid.*, p. 3.

Monopoly by the State is not fought simply by asserting monopoly by the family. " The schools do not belong exclusively to the State, nor to the private associations which conduct them, nor finally exclusively to society itself. Each agent according to its proper competence and within the limits of justice and equity has its own proper interest in the education of students. " [44]

Whether the Catholic position on the agencies of education is viewed merely from the writings of Pius XI or from the conciliar period of Vatican II, no difficulties should be encountered accepting shared time education. If anything, the program receives implicit encouragement through the frequent citations calling for harmony between the agencies of education, and for mutual acceptance of the rights of the Church, the family, and the State in education. Shared time would be in harmony with the view of Pius XI since the State serves as a supplementary agent to the family and the Church.

A new trend, however, is encountered in the conciliar period. Both the Church and the State serve to supplement the family in education. Even in regard to religious training, the burden is placed upon the parents and the Church too serves to assist the parents. There is then a definite acceptance that the State has assumed a major burden in education, and neither the Church, nor the family, nor the State has monopoly.

There is also the question of a pluralistic society. In such a society, which today is becoming common

[44] *Ibid.*

even outside the United States, what agency would non-Catholic parents turn to for fulfilling the educational needs of their children. Obviously, it would not be the Catholic Church. In a few cases it might be private educational institutions, but in reality it has been the public or State schools which have assumed the complete temporal education of the majority of children.

In the post-conciliar period there is definite emphasis placed upon the rights of parents. In calling for excellence in Catholic schools, the Fathers of the Council were often aware that this was not always the mark of each and every Catholic school. In such cases the Church has no right to request parents to send their children to Catholic schools alone, especially when the religious training of the child might be cared for by the parents themselves or through other programs designated by them.

Aside from these observations, the post-conciliar period requires mutual cooperation between the agencies of education. The rights of parents, the Church, and the State are encouraged and protected. Shared time activity not only appears to be in conformity with Vatican II thinking but seems made to order for this time of renewal and rethinking in the Catholic Church.

Case histories

For the past forty years, and especially within the past five or six years, shared time programs have sprouted throughout the country, with many more on the planning boards. In communities as distant and disparate as Bangor, Maine; Dewitt, Iowa; and Salem, Oregon, Catholics have seen fit to cooperate with the public schools in providing for the education needs of thousands of children.

The grandfather of the program may well be the shared time plan in Hartford, Connecticut. For more than thirty years Hartford has had a shared time arrangement. The Catholic school pupils come to the public school for instruction in industrial arts (for seventh and eighth grade boys) or home economics (for seventh and eighth grade girls). The number of pupils in each case is reported to the several public school principals by the Catholic schools early in the calendar year. The schedules are worked out cooperatively by the principals of each school and by the city coordinator for the special subject. The subjects are taught during a double period once a week. The instruction in the public school is offered by the public school subject. During the 1960-61 school year there were 487 girls and 466 boys from nine Catholic schools taking part in the program. No particular difficulty was experienced in scheduling. [1]

In Philadelphia, public and Catholic school officials have started shared time. In September of 1963, tenth grade pupils from twelve Catholic high schools in Philadelphia enrolled for vocational courses not offered in Catholic schools. They attend half of each day in the public schools and the other half in Catholic schools. Eight hundred Catholic students have expressed interest in taking the vocational courses. Pupils have to arrange their own transportation and take the regular exam for public technical schools. Courses include practical nursing, welding, plumbing, and machine shop. [2]

At the start of the 1963 school year, the Cherry Hill district in suburban Detroit began a bold program of shared time. C. P. Titus, administrative assistant to the superintendent of Southfield schools in which Cherry Hill is located reports that so far the plan is working out well. Under the program 182 seventh and eighth graders attending St. Norbert's elementary school go to the public school for a half-day session. The students take classes in mathematics, science, music, shop, arts and crafts, homemaking, and physical education. In the Catholic school they receive instruction in language, arts, social studies, and religion. " The children adapt readily to the pluralistic society in which they live by attending both schools, " Titus said. " The

---

[1] Stearns, *Shared Time—A Symposium*, p. 36.

[2] " Philadelphia to Try Shared Time, " *Cleveland Catholic Universe Bulletin*, XC (June 21, 1963), p. 1.

parochial students enjoy both schools. The public school students like to have their friends and neighbors become part of their school. " Titus emphasized that the " most important ingredient in a shared time program is the desire on the part of both the public school and the parochial school personnel for such a program. " [3] There are over four communities in Michigan with some type of shared time program. Menominee, Michigan, has had a shared time program for forty years.

The shortest distance between public and Catholic schools is probably the walk taken daily by eighty-two boys and girls at Michigan's Cheboygan Catholic High School. The walk is so short that the interval between classes has been cut from five to three minutes, since that is all the time needed ro leave an English or history class and get to the public school for other classes. For the past sixteen years, in this small, northern Michigan town, Catholic high school students have taken public school courses. Without realizing it, this was a pioneer venture into shared time.

The Rev. Robert Heyer, director of the Cheboygan Catholic High School, who has guided the Catholic end of the shared time since 1952, points out that the program needs, " constant watching so that harmony is not shattered. " [4] He has managed to do this with three different public school

[3] Maurine Hoffman, " Detroit Suburb Tried Shared Time, " *Washington Post* (February 24, 1964), p. 5.

[4] Edward Wakin, " Shared Time, " *Sign*, XLII (June, 1963), pp. 19-21.

superintendents. When problems arise, Heyer and the superintendent from the public school sit down and discuss solutions, striving to remember that their basic commitment as educators is the same— the best possible education for every child.

In Cheboygan, the Catholic students are taking both academic and vocational courses. The academic include physics, chemistry, trigonometry, solid geometry, and speech. The vocational include wood shop, metal shop, advanced mechanical drawing, and home economics. Sixty-two students are also taking driving training. The Catholic students are officially part-time members of the public school and the State of Michigan allows funds for them as it does for any student. Since the Catholic students are taking a total of 120 courses and four courses are regarded as equivalent to one student, the public school receives S⁺ate funds for an additional 30 students.

The two school bodies are well integrated sharing the social and athletic programs of both schools. The public school newspaper allots three pages of news to the Catholic school which does not have its own paper. The public school counsellor assists the Catholic students in choosing careers and colleges.

The Sister-principal handles scheduling of classes in this way: she begins by recording the schedule of the public school classes which her students will attend and then organizes the Catholic school schedule around them. But the Catholic school must accept the fact that public school students have preference and the Catholic school students can take classes only if there is room. A scheduling conflict must always be resolved in favor of the public school.

> The Cheboygan community views both schools as its own, even to the extent of having an annual civic luncheon to honor the athletes of both schools. To prevent tension from arising, no games or contests are scheduled between the two schools. They even avoid playing the same opponents, so comparisons are impossible. In the long run, Father Heyer's view has been confirmed: The kids themselves sell the program. [5]

Thirty-eight pupils from one and twenty-five from another parochial high school attend two public high schools in Bay City, Michigan. These pupils take trigonometry, drafting, vocational education, Spanish, and homemaking at the public high school. In Flint, Michigan, 187 Catholic school pupils from the seventh to the tenth grades attend public school for algebra, trigonometry, chemistry, physics, Spanish, and French. Public school buses are used for transportation.

In Shorewood, Wisconsin, the shared time program began thirty-four years ago. Over a third of Shorewood's 17,000 population is Catholic. A coordinating council of Catholic and public school officials met in 1930 and arranged for public school instruction in industrial arts and home economics. The Catholic school is five blocks from the public school. The pupils are unsupervised when they travel between schools. Catholic school pupils are

[5] *Ibid.*

in separate classes, and Shorewood receives no State aid for part-time pupils.

Jamestown, North Dakota, public schools enroll 3,300 pupils. Shared time has been practiced for twenty years. In 1964, 129 Catholic school pupils walked a block and a half to the public school for classes in foreign languages, science, and business and commercial subjects. The Catholic school children are placed in classes with the regular public school pupils. Since the parochial school pupils take an average of two subjects each, State aid, which requires enrollment in at least three subjects each, is not provided for them.

In September of 1964, Colton, Washington, opened the first shared time program in the State. The program has been operating with quiet efficiency in this small town near Spokane with school board and Church leaders pleased with the results. Most of Colton's families are Catholic. Enrolled in the Colton public elementary school are fifty-one students and in the Guardian Angel parochial school, one hundred and twenty-seven. In 1963 the superintendent of the Colton school district, Eugene Coate, asked State authorities to approve a shared time program. Meeting no opposition he estabished a program with Catholic officials.

As the plan works now, parochial school students in the fifth and sixth grades attend afternoon classes at the public school on Tuesdays and Thursdays while those in the seventh and eighth grades go to the public school on Mondays, Wednesdays, and Fridays. At the public school the parochial school students study subjects such as home economics, band, art, and shop, which are not available at their own school. They are also eligible to participate in such auxiliary services as guidance, speech therapy, the hot lunch program, and transportation.

In Monroeville, Pennsylvania, outside Pittsburgh, some thirty-six students from three Catholic high schools spend half the school day at the new Forbes Trail Area Technical School, studying such courses as marketing, chemistry, computers, engineering, and auto mechanics, and half their day at the Catholic high school studying religion, English, mathematics, social studies, and languages.

Bishop John McDowell, Superintendent of Schools for the Diocese of Pittsburgh, considers that the experiment at Forbes Trail has progressed far beyond expectations, while favorable comment has also come from Francis J. Brown, director of the school. Plans are being made for another shared time program in which the entire freshman class of a Pittsburgh Catholic high school will go to a nearby public school for instructions in mathematics, foreign languages, industrial arts, commercial subjects, and physical education. The Catholic students will continue to take courses in English, science, social studies, fine arts and religion at the Catholic high school.

In the Archdiocese of Chicago, Bishop William McManus, Superintendent of Schools, has long been an advocate of shared time. The archdiocese has over 65,000 enrolled in its Catholic high schools and is expanding its facilities as rapidly as financial resources and available qualified teachers allow.

However, nearly 50,000 Catholic children attend public high schools and there is no hope of making room for them in Catholic schools without resort to shared time programs. The John F. Kennedy public high school and the new St. Paul's high are engaged in the first shared time program in the city. It is hoped that eventually similar programs can be worked out whereby Catholic students will take their non-religious subjects in the public schools.

The pattern repeats itself through the country. The States that have some type of shared time program include Arizona, Arkansas, California, Colorado, Connecticut, Florida, Georgia, Illinois, Indiana, Iowa, Kansas, Kentucky, Louisiana, Massachusetts, Michigan, Minnesota, Mississippi, Missouri, Montana, Nebraska, New Jersey, New York, North Dakota, Ohio, Oklahoma, Oregon, Pennsylvania, South Dakota, Tennessee, Texas, Vermont, Washington, West Virginia, Wisconsin, and Wyoming.

From a practical consideration, shared time programs do work. However, if there is one lesson taught by successful shared time programs, it is the need for cooperation, cooperation between the two schools, between the parents and the two schools, and between the students and their two schools. It is because of the student that shared time exists, and it will be principally through the student that there will be an ever widening hole in the old fashioned wall which separates America's two great educational systems, the schools of the State and the schools of the Church.

There are problems

Shared time education is not without its critics or its problems. Though the opponents and their objections are diffuse, the difficulties related to the activity arise from three principal sources: the objections of Catholics, administrative problems, and lastly, the problems of legality.

Strange as it may appear the loudest Catholic voices against shared time have been those of parents. The parents' group opposing shared time is Citizens for Educational Freedom, a group consisting of approximately thirty thousand families and group members in the United States. Some of the groups include over a thousand members. The organization, composed largely of Catholics but non-denominational in scope, supports the rights of parents to make a free choice in selecting a school for the education of their children. Although neutral on the question of federal aid to education, it should benefit all children whether they attend a public or Catholic school. There should be shared taxes and shared benefits. [1]

[1] U.S. House of Representatives, *Hearings before the Ad Hoc Subcommittee on Study of Shared Time Education of the Committee on Education and Labor on H.R. 6074*, 88th Congress, 2nd Session, February 24, 25, 28, and March 11, 1964, p. 474.

Mark Murphy, a former national president of the Citizens for Educational Freedom, has stated the organization's general dissatisfaction with shared time. CEF believes that shared time is unworkable in the overwhelming majority of schools and, therefore, is not a practical plan to help the education of all children. There are other possibilities, involving less money, that could be adopted immediately to give better aid to more students. According to Murphy, the shared time program has failed to grow and not one activity has reached a substantial percentage of the total number of students in any single community in the United States. The failure of shared time has not been the lack of funds. Shared time has so many administrative obstacles that it can be programmed in only a very few places and is physically limited to a very few schools and a very few classes.

The CEF feels that the shared time concept adheres to the philosophy that the Federal Government should grant aid only to the public school. The parents' rights to choose either a public or religious school are ignored.

The most stinging criticism of shared time has come from Mrs. Jerome K. Beard, a Michigan CEF member, one of those whose daughters attended St. Norbert School and spent half of each day in Cherry Hill Public School. She stated:

> The whole situation is very confusing to my daughter. For half the school day her education is God-centered and the discipline very firm. For the other half, her education is not God-centered, with a more

permissive discipline which is at odds with my own convictions about the upbringing of my child. A child this age cannot sort out the differences in these values. When my daughter walks through the door of the public school, the government becomes interested in helping with her education. However, when she is in the school that I have chosen for her... the government is not interested in helping her, even though both of these schools are State approved and even though she learns subjects required by the State at the parochial school. [2]

However, when the Johnson administration's aid to education bill appeared in Congress with its provisions for shared time education, the Citizens for Educational Freedom supported the measure but felt that it left much to be desired. Stuart Hubbel, president of the CEF, testified before the House Subcommittee on Education that the organization supported the bill as a bona fide effort in the right direction as long as there were safeguards stipulating that there should be participation in local planning by nonpublic school authorities. [3]

The idea of shared time has been quite alarming to some Catholic teaching sisters. A number have felt that there would be a dislocation of teachers. The problem would be much greater at the level of the secondary than of the elementary school since the elementary teacher is much more of a generalist.

[2] John J. Daly, "Shared Time Schooling Critized as Unworkable," *Washington Catholic Standard*, XIV (March 20, 1964), 9.
[3] "Citizens for Educational Freedom Uphold LBJ Plan," *Boston Pilot*, February 3, 1965, 3.

The problem concerns the teachers who teach mathematics, science, etc., in fact any of the disciplines which are to be taught in the public schools. What will become of these teachers when shared time no longer permits them to teach their specialities?

The answer is simple. First of all a change to shared time will be gradual, and probably limited. In no way is there any implication in the shared time concept that each and every school will be involved in the activity. Specialists in certain areas could be sent to those schools which retained a total commitment to education. Second, little dislocation takes place if shared time is adopted since the teachers and facilities involved are those which Catholic schools do not have in sufficient abundance. The shortages are so great that it is questionable whether there will ever be an abundance of teachers or facilities in the future. Third, many of the younger teachers could be trained for college teaching or for newer forms of the apostolate where their specialities would be of value to the Church. At the same time many religious could be sent to major in theology and in religious education, using their previous specialities as an integrating factor with their colleagues in other disciplines.

A few Catholics have looked upon the Church's acceptance of shared time as an admission of failure in the efforts to obtain federal aid. However, Monsignor Neil D'Amour, Superintendent of Schools for the Diocese of Marquette, Michigan, has warned that shared time has no relationship to the question of federal aid for children attending Catholic Schools. [4]

Virgil C. Blum, professor of political science at Marquette University, Milwaukee, Wisconsin, has viewed President Johnson's education bill and shared time as establishing a principle which is more important to Catholic schools than the amount of aid the bill would provide. The education bill establishes the principle that all children should share in educational funds. " Based on this principle, we can hope that in the years ahead America, like almost every other democracy in the world, will provide tax funds for the education of Church-related school children in secular subjects. " [5]

A second problem related to shared time is administration. To fully implement the concept of shared time involves administrative reorganization of major proportions. Much will depend upon trial-and-error. Some communities will adapt more easily than others. In many States laws will have to be changed to permit basic enrollment in public schools for State aid purposes on a part time rather than full time pupil day. Allocation of basic enrollment, transfers of credit, arrangements for promotion and graduation are a few of the difficult problems which must be solved.

In the communities attempting shared time,

[4] Research Division—National Education Association, *Shared Time Programs: An Exploratory Study*, Research Report 1964-R 10 (1964), p. 18.
[5] " Jesuit Educator Declares Aid Bill Sets Principle, " *Boston Pilot* (February 13, 1965), p. 10.

three major areas of adjustment will be met: the allocation of building space, the lengthening and apportionment of school time, and the problem of scheduling of pupils and personnel. As far as public school instruction is concerned this will be given chiefly in publicly owned buildings under public jurisdiction and the Church school instruction will be given in Church-owned structures. An inventory must be made in each community of the suitable space available for each enterprise. In many communities no more parochial school building might be required. It may also be assumed that with extensive education plants of many Protestant church buildings, largely idle except on week-ends, many communities would find an inventory of ample Protestant facilities, especially if sharing and cooperative plans were to be developed.

All educational plant inventories should be formulated in terms of at least eleven-month and possible twelve-month usage each year. Numerous communities will find on this basis that existing plants will be sufficient for shared time activity. However, with an impending growth in school age population, some communities will probably need more public schools.

In many instances, in order to implement shared time, the school day will have to be lengthened and the public schools will have to be in session around the year. Some discussion in this direction already has taken place for the purpose of greater plant utility. This does not mean that more time will be required of the individual child, although some

Protestant and Jewish children will spend more time under religious instruction than many now do. It is to be hoped that increased emphasis and greater facility for scheduling will bring about a greater religious instruction among unchurched youth.

Perhaps the most difficult administrative task will be the scheduling of the school program. Many will cry " wolf " before the task is started. For those who maintain the status quo, the answer will be—impossible. Yet the genius of school administrators in adapting schedules has enabled the accomplishment of even the most impossible tasks. Scheduling has changed, is now undergoing change, and will continue to change.

Cooperative planning by public school and Church leaders must be expected. Experimentation on the secondary level in core programs, team teaching, and organization of courses into units and blocks may all serve in adjusting to shared time.

Where shared time has taken place on a limited scale, the Catholic schools have tried to accommodate themselves to the public schools. Public schools have given priority to their own student body and have not been forced to turn normal schedules upside down. No insurmountable scheduling problems have been reported. The fundamental problem is the willingness to work together and public acceptance locally of shared time. However, cooperation must take place on the part of both Catholic and public school administrators. The program will not succeed if the cooperation is one-sided.

A few practical administrative problems in shared time may be considered. With a child attending both a Catholic and public school, who grants the diploma? The practice is that the boy or girl graduates with a diploma from the parochial school. When the student applies for college, he is regarded as a graduate of the parochial school and his record, rank, and grades are determined by the Catholic school. In regard to the student's social and recreational activities, the parochial school student only attends classes in the public school. All other aspects of his school life are within the context of his parochial school.

In Harbor Beach, Michigan, where shared time education takes place between Harbor Beach Community High School and Our Lady of the Lake Huron High School, cooperation has been the key to success for administrative problems. The unusual report card issued between the two schools lists the Catholic high school grades in blue ink and those from the public school in red ink. Early semester exams are arranged in the public school so that Catholic students may go on retreat. The nuns are invited to in-service training sessions at the public school, and parents of shared time students are invited to the Parent-Teacher Conference Day.

All facilities of the public school are available to the students from the Catholic school, including the library and the labs. They can even join the clubs at the public school. A special section of public school books is also maintained at the Catholic school library.

The third and final problem related to shared time is the legality or constitutionality of the program. The problem has reference for both the federal and State constitutions. The ultimate decision in reference to the legality of shared time will have to come from the Supreme Court, if and when the program is attacked. However, various notions favoring or opposing the legality of the program have been discussed.

Leo Pfeffer, the legal counsel of the American Jewish Congress and the foremost authority among the strict separationists, has stated that, although there might be some objections to shared time on policy grounds, he believes the plan to be constitutional.

> In 1925, the Supreme Court ruled that a State could not forbid children from obtaining their entire secular education in parochial schools. In view of this decision I cannot see how an arrangement whereby children receive only half their secular education in parochial schools could be held unconstitutional. Moreover, in Zorach vs. Clauson (1952), the Court ruled that it is constitutionally permissible to release children from public school for part of the school day in order that they may receive religious instruction in Church schools. It would therefore seem doubly clear that releasing children for secular instruction would not violate the Constitution. [6]

Francis Chase, professor of education at the University of Chicago, and former dean of its

[6] Quoted in Louis Cassels, " A Way Out of Our Parochial— Public School Conflict, " *Look*, XXVI (August 28, 1962), p. 62.

Graduate School of Education, does not regard shared time centers as advocated in the Johnson administration education program as violating the wall of separation between Church and State if the centers are wisely administered as a community service. " The case seems to me little different from the use of tax-supported libraries, museums, and parks by those from schools of all kinds. " [7]

Harry L. Stearns, the father of shared time, questions those people who think that shared time is an aid to Catholic schools because it releases them from part of their financial burden. This is an incorrect interpretation for it presumes that parochial schools have a responsibility for education. In reality, this is the responsibility of the public schools. " Really (under shared time) public schools would be accepting their full responsibility. Any child who is a resident of a school district is entitled to attend its public schools. " [8]

The American Civil Liberties Union has divided sentiments among its members regarding shared time. The Union's national Church-State committee issued a statement in January 1965, as a recommendation for the many affiliates. In part the committee states that shared time does not " inherently result in constitutional or civil liberties violations involving the principles of the First Amendment's guarantee of mutual independence between religion and gov-

[7] Francis S. Chase, " Education Plan Is Like an LBJ Embrace, " *Washington Post* (January 17, 1965), p. E 3.

[8] " Educators See No Barriers In Shared Time Program, " *Boston Pilot* (March 28, 1964), 10.

ernment. " ⁹ However, constitutional principles will not necessarily require that shared time programs be offered by all schools or hinder a school board from reasonably finding that it cannot offer its facilities for the program without impairment of its total educational program. ¹⁰

The committee then sets forth some principles which are essential for the constitutional validity of shared time. The most obvious principle is that the program be offered on a non-discriminatory basis to all who reside within the school district. In other words, the program should be offered to parochial school children of every denomination. This does not preclude the establishment of reasonable classification of students or reasonable entrance requirements. " For instance, a public school might reasonably admit to part-time studies on a tuition paying basis non-residents of its districts who are students of a parochial school from which resident students are admitted to free part-time enrollment. " ¹¹

Essential to the validity of the program is the requirement that control be vested in public authority. This does not prevent cooperation between public and parochial school officials to ensure that the offering of public school facilities is made with knowledge of the needs of the private school

⁹ The Committee's Recommendation, " Shared Time and Civil Liberties: A Discussion, " *Civil Liberties—Monthly Publication of the American Civil Liberties Union* (January, 1965), p. 5.

¹⁰ *Ibid.*

¹¹ *Ibid.*

students. Ascertaining the needs of the private school students does not imply a commitment that the public school can and must meet each of these needs, for instance, that it will schedule its offerings to ensure accommodation of every religious holiday for which recognition is sought. Public control implies that decisions must be made by public officials and precludes delegation of authority to groups in which officers of parochial schools participate, over such matters as the selection of curricula, texts, of course objectives, the selection and tenure of teachers, or the direction of their work.

Shared time programs are to serve public rather than religious objectives. It would not be improper for public school authorities in making decisions concerning the size of new schools to take into account the anticipated part-time enrollment of students attending private and parochial schools. [12]

Byron Miller, a member of the American Civil Liberties Union Illinois Division's Board of Directors, opposes shared time. According to Miller, there have been few pure programs of shared time, and once the program is in full operation, there is a high potential for constitutional abuses. [13]

Related to this is Miller's conviction that the parochial school essentially controls the scope of shared time since the program reflects its omissions and the public school must offer all courses. The

[12] *Ibid.*

[13] Byron S. Miller, " A Statement of Opposition, " *Civil Liberties—Monthly Publication of the American Civil Liberties Union* (January 5, 1965), pp. 5-6.

public school administrator will be dependent upon parochial school decisions to avoid over- or under-staffing and to achieve feasible scheduling. Such dependence can also create effective pressure on controversial matters in the public school curriculum.

> Shared time requireclose interchange between Church and State. In this interchange, religious education, which is the reason for the existence of the Church schol is at odds with the permissible scope of the public school. It will provoke at least Church-State control conflicts if not actual Church control. [14]

Finally, Miller fears that shared time will bring with it the eventual weakening of the influences of the public schools. The teaching of the value courses such as history, civics, the humanities, and the social sciences, will be withdrawn from the public schools, and there will be a proliferation of part-time private schools. Since these are low-cost subjects, many such schools can be anticipated. Even in subjects left to the public school, the influence of private school administrations serving the same students will far exceed the present community influences. With the strength of the public schools weakened, there will be a loss of freedom, for " liberty without free, unfettered educational opportunity, without an informed (not indoctrinated) electorate, is a shadow. " [15] The whole democratic way of life in this country is

[14] *Ibid.*, p. 6.
[15] *Ibid.*

dependent upon the vital school system responsible to the electorate. [16]

Theodore Powell, a member of the Connecticut American Civil Liberties Union, and an early advocate of, and a prolific writer about shared time, sees no violation of the Constitution because children attend public school part-time. " What part of the Constitution requires that public education or any other public service must be offered on an all or nothing basis? " [17]

Powell questions those who fear that shared time would assist or promote religious education. There could be an improper administration of shared time, but unreasonable discrimination is possible in the administration of any government program. This is an argument against bad administration and not against shared time. Proper guidelines should be followed by administrators. [18]

On the federal level there have been no decisions by the Supreme Court dealing with shared time or cooperative practices in education. It would be impossible to draw conclusions from decisions concerning released time, free textbooks, transportation, State supervision of sectarian education, etc. However, in October of 1967, the Supreme Court agreed to decide sometime in 1968 whether taxpayers could bring lawsuits challenging federal education pro-

[16] *Ibid.*

[17] Theodore Powell, " Full Support for Shared Time, " *Civil Liberties—Monthly Publication of the American Civil Liberties Union* (January, 1965), p. 6.

[18] *Ibid.*

grams, especially assistance under Titles I and II of the 1965 law, which was based on the child benefit theory.

In very few jurisdictions has the legality of shared time programs been either tested in the courts, or ruled on in an opinion by a State attorney general. In fact only one high State court decision has been made directly on the point of shared time, and there exists only a handful of opinions by various State attorneys general.

The one, noteworthy court decision by the highest State court in Pennsylvania ruled in 1913 that the benefits and advantages of public schools as means of education and improvement are not restricted to the pupils in regular attendance and that the plaintiff, a seventh grade pupil at St. John's Parish school in Altoona, could not be denied access to the services of Pennsylvania public schools. The decision reads: " No pupil shall be refused admission to the courses in these additional schools or departments, by reason of the fact that his elementary education is being or has been received in a school other than a public school. " [19]

In 1962, the Wisconsin Supreme Court in *Reynolds vs. Nusbaum*, while ruling that State provision of bus transportation was unconstitutional, commented in passing that shared time was permissible. Although parochial pupils could constitutionally attend manual training and domestic science classes in public schools without cost, this did not

[19] Research Division—National Education Association, *op. cit.*, p. 14.

sustain the constitutionality of a statute affording nonpublic school pupils free bus transportation. [20]

In 1962, Oklahoma's attorney general gave legal endorsement to shared time on the basis of his State's law.   In the State of New York the legal officer of the State Department of Education ruled shared time as constituting unconstitutional aid to a religious school.   In California the attorney general found partial support for shared time in the law of the State.   The Utah attorney general ruled in favor of shared time as it applied to driver's education.   The New Jersey school board attorney endorsed shared time, citing the approval of the attorney general in Oregon, and the attorney for the school board of Dewitt, Iowa.   However, in 1962, the school board attorney in Clinton, Iowa, only nine miles from Dewitt, ruled that private school pupils cannot enroll part-time in public schools, and the State superintendent of public instruction in Iowa stated that the attendance of parochial high school pupils in public schools for courses in vocational homemaking or industrial arts is illegal in the State. [21]

In 1963, Oregon's attorney general's opinion stating that Catholic school children could attend public schools on a part-time basis was endorsed by the State board of education.   In March 1964, Maryland's attorney general ruled that public school facilities could be used by parochial school pupils for

[20] U.S. House of Representatives, *Hearings before the Ad Hoc Subcommitte on Study of Shared Time Education of the Committee on Education and Labor on* H.R. 6074, p. 238.

[21] *Ibid.*, p. 331.

secular education. In December 1964, the attorney general of the State of Washington ruled that the State had no legal barriers against shared time programs. The decision to initiate the program should be left to school boards.

The problem of legality as applied to the individual States is complex and without pattern. Obviously, State laws can be changed, and concerted efforts on the part of shared time advocates could be directed toward this effort.

It would appear that State provision precluding shared time in no way would affect President Johnson's education program. James E. Allen, State commissioner of education in New York, expressed the opinion that parochial and other private school pupils in the State of New York could legally partake in the federal program, despite the State constitution's ban against the use of public funds for non-public schools. Federal funds could be channeled through the State for parochial school children. The State would serve only as an administrative agency, and not a determining one. " It would not determine where the money was going, but only follow the recommendations of the Federal Government. "[22]

The Congress, the President, and the Department of Justice have made the judgment that shared time education does not violate the First Amendment of the Constitution. The United States Supreme Court has had no occasion to rule on the constitu-

[22] N. Y. Charter Not Violated, " *Register* " (January 24, 1965), p. 1.

tionality of the program. It is admitted that there could be difficulties and abuses in the fulfilling of shared time. The heaviest burden of steering a safe constitutional course will fall upon those who administer the program, whether they are in parochial or public school education. Perhaps the words of the astute Frenchman Alexis de Tocqueville have special bearing today: " I have never been more struck by the good sense and the practical judgment of the Americans than in the manner in which they elude the numberless difficulties resulting from their Federal Constitution. " [23]

[23] Quoted in John E. Vanderstar, " The Razor's Edge of Church-State, " *Washington Post* (April 4, 1965), p. E 3.

The two-edged sword

In itself shared time education serves as a two-edged sword. On the part of the Church it recognizes that the State has not merely the right to educate, independent of the Church, but a proper mission and role in education. On the part of the State there is established the precedent for public school educators that Catholic schools are not merely accepted, but are actual partners with State schools. For the first time there is official, national and local recognition that Catholic schools are an integral part of the American educational way of life.

With the establishment of shared time education Catholic education has reached a plateau. There are still challenges facing Catholic educators. Old concepts and approaches in Catholic education will have to be re-examined and educators will have to be prepared to inaugurate revolutionary ideas and to work closely with public school authorities.

The most important task facing Catholic school administrators is to establish strong lines of communication with public school authorities. This will not always be easy since religious educators approach education in ways which are, in significant part, different from public school educators. The Catholic educator is committed to a philosophy of education, and in fact to a theology of education, which considers every aspect of the child's nature in the formulation of educational experiences. Consequently, religion is of prime importance and ultimately all experiences must be viewed and interpreted in terms of the child's relationship with God. This distinguishes a religiously-oriented education from public education.

The public school educator is committed to a different philosophy of education. Because of the American pluralistic society, formal religious instruction has become impossible. The public school may teach about religion but it may not teach religion. Certain elements in fact are even dedicated to the proposition that the public school is and must be in every sense a secular institution. Every trace of religious practices and traditions are being attacked. The trend is clearly directed toward a completely neutral public school and this is being confirmed by decisions of State and federal courts.

The vast majority of public school educators are not secularists and in fact numerous religiously-oriented men and women are holding teaching positions in public schools. These educators are not unaware of the role of religion in the formation of the child. If anything, the majority are quite aware of the importance of religion in the educational process and are faced with a dilemma which confronts them as loyal public school teachers in a religiously pluralistic society.

In the past, the Catholic educator might have preferred to see every Catholic child in a Catholic school, from kindergarten to the university, and he would have liked to have every educational experience related to man's ultimate and fundamental relationship to God. Yet the Catholic educator cannot ignore the existential reality that this ideal has not been, nor will it ever be, achieved. In fact, in viewing the changing times and the secularization of the temporal order, the Church can no longer afford to direct her mission of service to formal education alone. Nevertheless, the fact remains that an increasing number of Catholic children are denied even a minimum education in the faith.

The Catholic cannot be unconcerned about the rise and spread of religious illiteracy among non-Catholics. Far too many American children are receiving little, and in fact some, no religious instruction at all. Without exposure to the things of God, there can be no knowledge of God, and without knowledge there can be no love and worship. The loser, of course, is the child. However, the nation suffers because of the rise of irreligion. The American democratic way of life depends upon the acceptance of certain fundamental religious truths and values. How long can a nation endure if these truths and values are allowed to die in the hearts of America's children.

Shared time education serves as a rainbow of hope at a moment in history when something dramatically different is needed to strengthen and preserve the American way of life with its spiritual and democratic foundations. Shared time may well be the way to strengthen the common good without invading any of the rights or ideals so sacred to Americans as individuals or as a nation. The program takes into consideration the rights of parents, the Church, and the State, while at the same time being realistic, allowing the rendering to God those things that are rightly His.

Shared time education acknowledges that the religious formation of the child is of singular importance and that it cannot be accomplished in a few hasty hours but that it deserves a systematic approach. It further recommends that there are other subjects in the curriculum, aside from religion, which for one reason or another, may be better presented in a religiously-oriented framework. The practical problems involved are countless, yet the principles which give meaning to shared time activity as well as the reasons which motivate the program are altogether praiseworthy.

Whatever happens to shared time, it represents a giant stride forward in the definition, individual and common, of the responsibilites of the parent, the Church, and the State. Although for numerous reasons, one may object to this startling, new and unique concept of education, it is hoped that the historic significance of the shared time concept is not lost and that its potential for the development of the nation and its children is not ignored.

Is shared time the answer to America's educational problems? It is difficult to answer simply yes or no. Whether one favors the program or not, shared time education stands on its own, for it recognizes that Americans do differ in their religious beliefs and the rights of parents, the Church and the State must not be neglected.

Let then the three agencies of education, the family, the Church, and the State, experiment and cooperate, cooperate and experiment. Only time will tell whether shared time education will turn out to be a successful American answer to a peculiarly American problem, but it is certainly worth thinking, working, and talking about. In any case the words immortalized by John Fitzgerald Kennedy in his inaugural address as President of the United States aptly describe the attitude invoked in this work:

" Let us begin. "

BIBLIOGRAPHY

PUBLIC DOCUMENTS

Acta et Decreta Concilii Plenarii Baltimorensis Terti, Baltimore: John Murphy, 1886.

Conciliorum Provincialium et Plenarii Baltimorensium, Decreta, Baltimore, 1853.

Second Vatican Council, *Constitution on the Church*, Washington: National Catholic Welfare Conference, 1964.

Supreme Court of the United States, *Opinions No. 468, October Term, 1961; Nos. 142 and 119, October Term, 1962*, Washington: U.S. Government Printing Office, 1963.

Understanding the Elementary and Secondary Education Act of 1965, Washington: Department of Education—National Catholic Welfare Conference, 1966.

U.S. House of Representatives, *Hearings before the Ad Hoc Subcommittee on Education and Labor on H.R. 6074*, 88th Congress: 2nd. Session, February 24, 25, 28; and March 11, 1964.

— *H.R. 2363—A Bill to Strengthen and Improve Educational Opportunities in the Nation's Elementary and Secondary Schools*, 89th Congress, 1st Session, January 12, 1965.

— *Message from the President of the United States Transmitting Education Program*, Document No. 45, 89th Congress.

BOOKS

Abbott, Walter (ed.), *The Documents of Vatican II*, New York: Guild-America, & Association Presses, 1966.

Ahern, Patrick Henry, *The Catholic University of America, 1887-1896—The Rectorship of John J. Keane*, Washington: Catholic University of America Press, 1948.

— *The Life of John J. Keane*, Milwaukee: Bruce, 1954.

Anderson, Floyd (ed.), *Council Daybook Vatican II, Session 3*, Washington: National Catholic Welfare Conference, 1965.

Barry, Colman, *The Catholic University of America, 1903-1909—The Rectorship of Denis J. O'Connell*, Washington: Catholic University of America Press, 1950.

Billington, Ray Allen, *The Protestant Crusade 1800-1860*, New York, 1938.

Bouquillon, Thomas, *Education: To Whom Does It Belong?* Baltimore: John Murphy, 1891.

— *Education: To Whom Does It Belong? A Rejoinder to Critics*, Baltimore: John Murphy, 1892.

Butts, Freeman, R. and Cremin, Lawrence A., *A History of Education in American Culture*, New York:Holt, Rinehart and Winston, 1961.

Callahan, Daniel (ed.), *Federal Aid and Catholic Schools*, Baltimore: Helicon Press, 1964.

Conway, James, *The Respective Rights and Duties of Family, State, and Church in Regard to Education*, New York: Pustet, 1890.

— The State Last: *A study of Doctor Bouquillon's Pamphlet*, New York: Pustet, 1892.

Costanzo, Joseph, *This Nation Under God*, New York: Herder and Herder, 1964.

Drinan, Robert F., *Religion, The Courts, and Public Policy*, New York: McGraw-Hill, 1963.

Drouin, Edmond G., *The School Question: A Bibliography on Church-State Relationships in American Education 1940-1960*, Washington: Catholic University of America Press, 1963.

Dubay, Thomas, *Philosophy of the State as Educator*, Milwaukee: Bruce, 1959.

Dunne, Edmund F., *Our Public Schools: Are They Free or Are They Not?* New York: Thomas Egan, 1875.

Ellis, John Tracy (ed.), *Documents of American Catholic History*, Milwaukee: Bruce, 1953.

— *The Formative Years of the Catholic University of America*, Washington: American Catholic Historical Association, 1946.

— *The Life of James Cardinal Gibbons*, Milwaukee: Bruce, 1952.

Ford, Paul L. (ed.), *The Writings of Thomas Jefferson*, 12 vols, New York: Putnam, 1906.

Goerner, E. A., *Peter and Caesar*, New York: Herder and Herder, 1965.

Hall, A. J., *Religious Education in New York*, Chicago, 1914.

Hardon, John A., *Christianity in Conflict: A Catholic View of Protestantism*, Westminster, Md.: Newman Press, 1959.

Hartnett, Robert C., *Equal Rights for Children*, New York: America Press, 1948.

— *Federal Aid to Education, the Rights of Children Attending Non-*

public Schools, A Sequel to "Equal Rights for Children," New York: America Press, 1950.

Hartnett, Robert C. (ed.), *The Right to Educate: Democracy and Religious Education—A Symposium,* New York: America Press, 1949.

Hogan, Peter E., *The Catholic University of America, 1896-1903—The Rectorship of Thomas J. Conaty,* Washington: Catholic University of America Press, 1949.

Holaind, R., *The Parent First: An Answer to Dr. Bouquillon's Query 'Education: To Whom Does It Belong?'* New York: Benziger Brothers, 1892.

Ireland, John, *The Church and Modern Society,* Chicago, 1897, I.

Janssens, Louis, *Freedom of Conscience and Religious Freedom,* Staten Island, New York: Alba House, 1966.

John XXIII, *Pacem in Terris,* Boston: St. Paul Editions, 1964.

Johnston, Herbert, *A Philosophy of Education,* New York: McGraw-Hill, 1964.

Kerwin, Jerome, *Catholic Viewpoint on Church and State,* Garden City, New York: Hanover House, 1960.

LaNoue, George R., *Public Funds for Parochial Schools?* New York: National Council of Churches, 1963.

Lord, Robert H.; Sexton, John E.; and Harrington, Edward T.; *History of the Archdiocese of Boston.* Vol. I, New York: Sheed and Ward, 1944.

Loughery, Bernard F., *Parental Rights in American Educational Law, Their Bases and Implementation,* 2nd. ed., Washington: Catholic University of America Press, 1957.

Love, Thomas T., *John Courtney Murray: Contemporary Church-State Theory,* Garden City, New York, Doubleday, 1965.

Maritain, Jacques, *Man and the State,* Chicago: University of Chicago Press, 1961.

McClure, A. K., *Recollections of Half a Century,* Salem, Mass., 1902.

McCluskey, Neil G. (ed.), *Catholic Education in America: A Documentary History,* New York: Teachers College, Columbia University, Classics in Education No. 21, 1964.

— *Catholic Viewpoint on Education,* Garden City, New York: Hanover House, 1959.

Murray, John Courtney, *We Hold These Truths,* New York: Sheed and Ward, 1960.

Neuwien, Reginald, (ed.), *Catholic Schools in Action,* Notre Dame: University of Notre Dame Press, 1966.

Oaks, Dallin H., *The Wall Between Church and State*, Chicago: University of Chicago Press, 1963.

Padover, Saul K. (ed.), *The Complete Jefferson*, New York: Duell, 1943.

— *Thomas Jefferson On Democracy*, New York: Appleton-Century, 1939.

Papal Teachings on Education, edited by the Benedictine Monks of Solesmes, trans. by Aldo Rebeschini, Boston: Daughters of St. Paul, 1960.

Phenix, Philip H., *Religious Concerns in Contemporary Education*, New York: Teachers College, Columbia University, 1959.

Power, Edward J., *Main Currents in the History of Education*, New York: McGraw, Hill, 1962.

Putnam, John F., and Tankard, George G., *Pupil Accounting for Local and State School Systems*, (State Educational Records and Reports Series: Handbook V, Bulletin No. 39), Washington: Government Printing Office, 1964.

Redden, John D. and Ryan, Francis A., *A Catholic Philosophy of Education*, Milwaukee: Bruce, 1956.

Reilly, Daniel, *The School Controversy*, Washington: Catholic University of America Press, 1943.

Reuter, George S., *Shared Time*, Chicago: American Federation of Teachers, 1963.

The Role of the Independent School in American Democracy, Milwaukee, Wis.: Marquette University Press, 1956.

Ryan, Mary Perkins, *Are Parochial Schools the Answer?* New York: Holt, Rinehart, and Winston, 1964.

Sanders, Thomas G., *Protestant Concepts of Church and State: Historical Backgrounds and Approaches for the Future*, New York: Holt, Rinehart and Winston, 1964.

Shaver, Erwin L., *The Weekday School Church*, Boston: The Pilgrim Press, 1956.

Thayer, V. T., *The Attack upon the American Secular School*, Boston: Beacon Press, 1951.

Tussman, Joseph (ed.), *The Supreme Court on Church and State*, New York: Oxford University Press, 1962.

Vatican Council II, New York: America Press, 1964.

Weigel, Gustave, *Church-State Relations—A Theological Consideration*, Baltimore: Helicon Press, 1960.

Wolf, Donald J. and Schall, James V., (eds.), *Current Trends in Theology*, Garden City, New York: Doubleday, 1965.

ARTICLES AND PERIODICALS

"Administrators Shy Away from Shared Facilities for Practical Reasons," *Nation's Schools*, LXIX (June, 1962), p. 70.

"Aid for All: Do State Public School Chiefs Want It?" *Register*, February 14, 1965, p. 3.

"All Schools, Cooperation Is Administration's Aim," *Cleveland Catholic Universe Bulletin*, XCI (January 29, 1965), p. 3.

Anderson, Walter A., "Shared Time: I'm Against It." *NEA Journal*, LIII (March, 1964), pp. 28-30.

Ball, William B., "The Johnson Education Bill," *Commonweal*, LXXXI (February 12, 1965), pp. 638-640.

Bayma, P., "The Liberalistic View of the Public School Question," *American Catholic Quarterly Review*, II (1877), pp. 1-29.

Billington, Ray Allen, "American Catholicism and the Church-State Issue," *Christendom*, V (Summer, 1940), pp. 355-366.

Bouquillon, Thomas, "The Apostolic Delegation," *American Catholic Quarterly Review*, XX (1895), pp. 112-31.

— "A Reply," *Educational Review*, III (April, 1892), pp. 365-73.

"Bp. Elwell Heartened by LBJ School Plan," *Cleveland Catholic Universe Bulletin*, January 15, 1965, p. 3.

Brownson, Orestes, "Public and Parochial Schools," *Brownson's Quarterly Review*, New York Series, IV (1859), p. 330.

Buder, Leonard, "Church-State Issue in New York," *New York Times*, April 10, 1966, p. E-7.

Canavan, Francis P., "Changing Jewish Attitudes," *America*, CXII (February 13, 1965), p. 214.

— "The New Education Bill," *America*, CXII (January 23, 1965), pp. 108-11.

— "The State as Educator," *Thought*, XXV (September, 1950), pp. 487-96.

Carper, Elsie, "Johnson School Bill Seen as Reconciling Religious Groups," *Washington Post*, January 29, 1965, p. 6.

— "Modification Urged on School Aid Bill," *Washington Post*, February 3, 1965, p. 8.

— "School Bill Defended on Church-State Issue," *Washington Post*, January 27, 1965, p. 1.

— "School Bill Stirs Angry Argument," *Washington Post*, January 30, 1965, p. 1.

— "3 Simultaneous Hearings Speed Progress of Education Package," *Washington Post*, February 2, 1965, p. 2.

Cassels, Louis, "A Way Out of Our Parochial-Public School Conflict," *Look*, XXVI, No. 18 (August 28, 1962), pp. 54-62.

— "LBJ Formula Avoids Church-State Hassle," *Boston Traveler*, January 13, 1965, p. 5.

"Catholic Education Official Urges Good Look At Shared Time," *Cleveland Catholic Universe Bulletin*, XC, No. 46 (February 28, 1964), p. 4.

Chase, Francis S., "Education Plan Is Like an LBJ Embrace," *Washington Post*, January 17, 1965, p. E-3.

Chatard, F. S., "Dr. Bouquillon on the School Question," *American Ecclesiastical Review*, VI (1892), pp. 98-103.

"The Child: Citizen of Two Worlds," Statement Issued by The Catholic Bishops of the United States, November, 1950. Text in Raphael M. Huber (ed.), *Our Bishops Speak, National Pastorals and Annual Statements of the Hierarchy of the United States, 1919-1951*, Milwaukee: Bruce, 1952, pp. 161-69.

"Citizens for Educational Freedom Uphold LBJ Plan," *Boston Pilot*, February 6, 1965, p. 3.

The Committee's Recommendation, "Shared Time and Civil Liberties: A Discussion," *Civil Liberties—Monthly Publication of the American Civil Liberties Union*, January, 1965, p. 5.

Connell, Francis J., "Christ the King of Civil Rulers," *American Ecclesiastical Review*, CXIX (October, 1948), p. 250.

"The Continuing Duel Over Dual Schooling," *Register*, XL, No. 8 (February 23, 1964), p. 7.

Daly, John J., "Religious Spokesmen Back School Aid Plan," *Washington Catholic Standard*, XV (February 5, 1965), p. 1.

— "Shared Time Schooling Criticized as Unworkable," *Washington Catholic Standard*, XIV (March 20, 1964), p. 9.

— "Some Church-State Bumps Fail to Derail LBJ's School Aid Bill," *Pilot*, February 13, 1965, p. 10.

Dawson, Christopher, "Education and the State," *Commonweal*, LXV (January 25, 1957), pp. 423-27.

Deedy, John G., "The Shared Time Experiment," *Commonweal*, LXXIX, No. 18 (January 13, 1964), pp. 530-32.

Degler, Carl N., "Aid for Parochial Schools—A Question of Education, Not Religion," *New York Times Magazine*, January 31, 1965, p. 11.

Dirks, J. E., "Should Religion Be Taught in Tax-Supported Colleges and Universities," *Christian Scholar*, XLV (Winter, 1962), pp. 259-66.

"Dissent on Shared Time," *America*, CVII (July 7, 1962), p. 453.

Dole, Kenneth, "Growth Predicted For Shared Time," *Washington Post*, March 2, 1963, p. 16.

Drinan, Robert F., "Ten Nations Discuss Freedom of Education," *America*, XCIII (September 3, 1955), pp. 526-28.

Driscoll, Justin A., "Shared Time Opposed," *Catholic Educator*, XXXII (June, 1962), p. 913.

"Education Proposals to Get Prompt Action," *Washington Catholic Standard*, XV (January 22, 1965), p. 1.

"Educator Expresses Fear Over Shared-Time Plan," *Register*, XL (August 9, 1964), p. 1.

"Educators See No Barriers In Shared-Time Program," *Boston Pilot*, March 28, 1964, p. 10.

Elliott, Walter, "The School Grievance and Its Remedy," *Catholic World*, XXXVI (1882-1883), pp. 713-17.

Ellis, John Tracy, "Church and State: An American Tradition," *Catholic Mind*, LII (April, 1954), pp. 209-16.

"Episcopalian Council Backs Education Bill," *Boston Herald*, February 18, 1965.

Fenton, Joseph C., "Principles Underlying Traditional Church-State Doctrine," *American Ecclesiastical Review*, CXXVI (June, 1952), pp. 452-62.

Finucan, J. Thomas, "Let's Give Shared Time a Try," *America*, November 13, 1965, pp. 568-70.

Fitzpatrick, Edward A., "Federal Government and the Schools," *Catholic School Journal*, LIX (March, 1959), pp. 67-69.

—— "The Right to Educate," *Catholic School Journal*, LVIII (March, 1958), pp. 27-29.

Fleming, Helen, "Catholics to Propose Shared School Plan to City," *Chicago Daily News*, September 17, 1962, p. 23.

Fleming, Arthur S., "The Shared Time Program Is Worth a Try," *Goodhousekeeping*, CLV (February, 1963), pp. 48-52.

Gallup, George, "49 % Favor Increase in Federal School Aid," *Washington Post*, March 7, 1965, p. 2.

Geoghegan, Arthur T., "Shared Time Plan Favored," *Catholic Educator*, XXXII (June, 1962), p. 913.

Grant, Gerald, "School Bill Aim Lauded by Prelate," *Washington Post*, January 28, 1965, p. A-31.

—— "Shared Time Test Urged by Keppel," *Washington Post*, February 29, 1964, p. 6.

— "Shared Time Might Be Key to Church School Aid Puzzle," *Washington Post*, February 17, 1963, p. E-2.

— "Superintendents Back School Aid Bill," *Washington Post*, February 18, 1965, p. 4.

Griswold, Erwin, "Griswold on Church-State," *America*, March 16, 1963, pp. 374-75.

Hoffman, Maurine, "Detroit Suburb Tries Shared Time," *Washington Post*, February 24, 1964, p. 5.

Hoffman, Maurine, and Grant, Gerald P., "Students of 1970 Will Find School Far Different If LBJ Plan Passes," *Washington Post*, January 14, 1965.

Holaind, R., "The Parent First:An Answer to Dr. Bouquillon's Query, 'Education: To Whom Does It Belong?'" *American Ecclesiastical Review*, VI (1892), pp. 75-76.

Holbrook, C. A., "Sectarianism, Pluralism, and Tax-Supported Institutions," *Christian Scholar*, XLV (Winter, 1962), pp. 290-300.

"How Big Is The Crisis For Catholic Schools?" *U.S. News & World Report*, LVI, No. 5 (February 3, 1964), pp. 60-64.

Hutchins, Robert M., "The Future of the Wall," *America*, January 26, 1963, pp. 146-49.

"In Memoriam, Thomas Joseph Bouquillon, 1840-1902," *Catholic University Bulletin*, IX (1903), pp. 153-63.

"Interfaith Conference Held on Shared Time," *Boston Pilot*, March 28, 1964, p. 10.

"Jesuit Educator Declares Aid Bill Sets Principle," *Pilot*, February 13, 1965, p. 10.

Kelley, Dean M., "Protestants and Parochial Schools," *Commonweal*, LXXIX, No. 18 (January 13, 1964), pp. 520-24.

Kerby, William J., "Bouquillon," *Dictionary of American Biography*. Educational Briefs, No. 6 (April, 1904), pp. 3-4.

— "Thomas Bouquillon," *Catholic Encyclopedia*, II, p. 716.

Knoff, Gerald E., "Fears Church Scramble for Aid: Shared Time Might Be Answer," *Nation's Schools*, April, 1963, p. 100.

LaNoue, George R., "Religious Schools and Secular Subjects," *Harvard Educational Review*, XXXII (Summer, 1962), pp. 255-291.

Legal Department—National Catholic Welfare Conference. "The Constitutionaloty of the Inclusion of Church-Related Schools in Federal Aid to Education," *The Georgetown Law Journal*, L (Winter, 1960), pp. 399-455.

Leo XIII, "Sapientiae Christianae," *Acta Santae Sedis*, XXII (1889-1890).

"Mass Enrollment Threat Spurs Shared-Time Study," *Register*, XL (September 13, 1964), p. 5.

McBee, Susanna, "Public School Aid Says Shared Time May End Conflict," *Washington Post*, February 20, 1963, p. 20.

McDowell, John B., "Shared Time," *C.E.A.P. Bulletin*, The Official Publication of the Catholic Educational Association of Pennsylvania, XVI, No. 3 (Summer, 1962), pp. 9-22.

McKenzie, John L., "The State in Christian Perspective," *Critic*, XXII (June-July, 1964), pp. 5-21.

McKeough, Michael J., " The State, the Church and the School," *Catholic Educational Review*, XLVII (May, 1949), pp. 291-302.

Miller, Arthur L., "Shared Time," *Parish Education Bulletin* (Lutheran Church, Missouri Synod), June, 1962, pp. 19-24.

Miller, Byron S., "A Statement of Opposition," *Civil Liberties— Monthly Publication of the American Civil Liberties Union*, January, 1965, pp. 5-6.

Moley, Raymond, "Federal School Aid-1," *Newsweek*, February 22, 1965, p. 100.

"Most Public School Leaders Favor Shared Time," *Cincinnati Catholic Telegraph*, July 16, 1964, p. 1.

Murray, John Courtney, "The Declaration on Religious Freedom: Its Deeper Significance," *America*, April 23, 1966, pp. 592-93.
— "The Problem of Pluralism in America," *Thought*, XXIX (Summer, 1954), pp. 165-208.
— "The Problem of Religious Freedom," *Theological Studies*, XXV (December, 1964), pp. 503-74.
— "Reflections on the Religiously Pluralistic Society," *Catholic Mind*, LVII (May-June, 1959), pp. 196-288.
— "The Religious School in a Pluralistic Society," *Catholic Mind*, LIV (September, 1956), pp. 502-11.
— "Separation of Church and State," *America*, LXXVI (December 7, 1946), pp. 261-63.
— "Separation of Church and State: True and False Concepts," *America*, LXXVI (February 15, 1947), pp. 541-45.
— "This Matter of Religious Freedom," *America*, CXII (January 9, 1965), pp. 40-44.

National School Public Relations Association. "Is Shared Time the Solution?" *Education U.S.A.*, February 27, 1964, p. 101.

National School Public Relations Association. "News Front," *Education U.S.A.*, April 2, 1964, p. 121.

"New Issue Faces Chicago Schools," *New York Times*, March 15, 1964, p. 52.

"N. Y. Charter Not Violated," *Register*, XLI (January 24, 1965), p. 1.

O'Gara, James, "A Chance for Shared Time," *Commonweal*, LXXX (April 17, 1964), p. 110.

— "Point and Counterpoint: Federal Funds and Shared Time," *Commonweal*, LXXVIII (May 10, 1963), p. 184.

— "Sharing the Time," *Commonweal*, LXXV (March 2, 1962), p. 586.

— "Sharing the Time," *Commonweal*, LXXV (March 9, 1962), p. 612.

Pfeffer, Leo, "Second Thoughts on Shared Time," *Christian Century*, June 20, 1961, pp. 779-80.

"Philadelphia To Try Shared Time," *Cleveland Catholic Universe Bulletin*, XC, No. 10 (June 21, 1963), p. 1.

Powell, Theodore, "Full Support for Shared Time," Civil Libertie. —*Monthly Publication of the American Civil Liberties Union*, January, 1965, p. 6.

— "Shared Time, I'm in Favor," *NEA Journal*, LIII (March, 1964), pp. 29-30.

— "The Shared Time Experiment, Is It Legal?" *Saturday Review*, XLVII (February 15, 1964), p. 69.

Power, Edward J., "The State and Catholic Education: Brownson, Spalding and Ireland," *Cithara*, I, No. 2 (May, 1962), pp. 24-36.

"President's Stress on 'Child' Praised," *Washington Catholic Standard*, XV (January 15, 1965), p. 1.

"A Program in Shared Time," *American School Board Journal*, XXLV (October, 1962), pp. 17-18.

"Protestant Group Backs Shared Time Education," *Boston Pilot*, June 13, 1964, p. 11.

Protestants and Other Americans United for Separation of Church and State. "Rough Time," *Church and State*, XVI (September, 1963), p. 9.

— "Shared Time Debated," *Church and State*, XVII (April, 1964), p. 17.

"The Public Schools—Threatened By Whom?" *Cleveland Catholic Universe Bulletin*, XC (May 17, 1963), p. 5.

Reed, George E., "Separation of Church and State: Its Real Meaning," *Catholic Action*, XXXI (March, 1949), pp. 9-11.

Regan, John J., " Religious Neutrality," *America*, January 18, 1964, pp. 74-76.

"Religion Courses Urged for Schools," *Boston Herald*, February 16, 1965, p. 3.

Reston, James, "Johnson Skirts Church-State Issue on Schools," *Boston Herald*, January 13, 1965.

Rice, Arthur H., "Are Shared Facilities the Answer?" *The Nation's Schools*, LXIX (June, 1962), pp. 54-57.

Salsinger, Harry, "Michigan Schools Open Era of Cooperation," *Washington Post*, December 12, 1965, p. M-14.

"Saxbee Says Shared Time Is Not Legal," *Cleveland Catholic Universe Bulletin*, XCI (January 29, 1965), p. 1.

"Schools and Vatican II," *America*, CXII (January 23, 1965), p. 97.

Schuster, Marjorie, "Shift of Pupils Won't Solve Race Issue, Elwell Says," *Cleveland Press*, August 31, 1963, p. 4.

"Serious Consideration for Shared Time," *Phi Delta Kappan*, XLIII (May, 1962), p. 337.

"Shared Facilities: School Administrators Opinion Poll Findings," *Nation's Schools*, LXIX (June, 1962), p. 70.

"Shared School Time Is Criticized at Hearing," *Washington Post*, March 12, 1964, p. B-2.

"Shared Services and Conscience," *America*, April 16, 1966, pp. 542-43.

"Shared Time," *Wall Street Journal*, June 20, 1963.

"Shared Time in Spotlight As Solution to School Aid," *Cleveland Catholic Universe Bulletin*, XCI (January 15, 1965), p. 1.

"Shared Time—Many Call It Best Answer," *Register*, XLI (January 31, 1965), p. 8.

"Shared Time Plan Faces Hectic Future," *Christian Century*, LXXXIX (March 14, 1962), pp. 317-18.

"Shared Time Plan Seen Working Well," *Washington Catholic Standard*, January 8, 1965, p. 2.

"Shared Time Program Tested Here," *Michigan Catholic* (Detroit), XCL (March 14, 1963), p. 1.

"Shared Time Programs," *La Crosse, Wis., Times-Review*, February 23, 1963, p. 1.

"Shared Time Success, School Heads Are Told," *Cleveland Catholic Universe Bulletin*, XC (February 28, 1964), p. 1.

Shaw, Russell, "CEF: They'd Rather Fight," *Sign*, November, 1965, pp. 13-16.

Shunk, William R., "Shared Time... New Light on an Old Problem?" *Phi Delta Kappan*, XLIII (June, 1962), pp. 377-79.

"Small Parish School Said Thing of Past," *Register*, XL (September 13, 1964), p. 1.

Speidel, Harold, "Shared Time," *Saturday Review*, XLVII (March 21, 1964), p. 63.

Stearns, Harry L., "Shared Time: Answer to an Impasse," *Christianity and Crisis*, XXI (September 18, 1961), pp. 154-57.

"The Teaching Mission of the Church," Statement issued by the Catholic Bishops of the United States, November 16, 1958, *Catholic Mind*, LVII (March-April, 1959), pp. 181-85.

"Two High Schools in Chicago Making Shared Time History," *Cleveland Catholic Universe Bulletin*, October 22, 1965, p. 15.

"Unitarian Group Hits Shared Time," *Cleveland Catholic Universe Bulletin*, XCI (January 15, 1965), p. 1.

Vanderstar, John E., "The Razor's Edge of Church-State," *Washington Post*, April 4, 1965, p. E-1.

Wakin, Edward, "Richard's Double School Life," *Sign*, March 1965, pp. 13-19.

Wakin, Edward, "Shared Time," *Sign*, XLII, No. 11 (June, 1963), pp. 19-21.

— "The Shared Time Experiment—How It Operates?" *Saturday Review*, February 15, 1964, p. 68.

Ward, Leo R., "Church and State, Their Possible Collaboration in Educational Areas Cited," *Catholic World*, CXCIX (April, 1964), p. 167.

Weclew, Robert G., "Church and State: How Much Separation?" *DePaul Law Review*, X (Autumn-Winter, 1960), pp. 1-26.

Weigel, Gustave, "Catholic and Protestant: End of War?" *Thought*, XXXIII (Autumn, 1958), pp. 383-97.

— "The Church and the Democratic State," *Thought*, XXVII (Summer, 1952), pp. 165-84.

"What Price Partnership?" *Newsweek*, February 22, 1965, p. 59.

Williams, George Hunston, " Church-State Separation and Religion in the Schools of Our Democracy," *Religious Education*, LI (September-October, 1956), pp. 369-77.

— "The Church, the Democratic State, and The Crisis in Religiou Education," *Harvard Divinity School Bulletin*, XLVI (1949) pp. 35-61.

Woodlock, Thomas F., "American Principles Versus Secular Education," *Catholic World*, LXXIX (1904), pp. 711-18.

Woelf, Paul A., "About Shared Time," *America*, CVII (April 28, 1962), p. 103.

Yanitelli, Victor R., (ed.), "A Church-State Anthology: The Work of Father Murray," *Thought*, XXVII (Spring, 1952), pp. 6-42.

REPORTS

National Catholic Educational Association. "The Right to Educate —The Role of Parents, Church, State," *National Catholic Educational Association Bulletin*—Proceedings, LV (August, 1958), pp. 1-416.

Nelson, Claud D. (ed.), *The Dialogue—Shared Time*. A Project of the National Conference of Christians & Jews, Bulletin No. 30, New York, 1964.

Research Division—National Education Association. *Shared-Time Programs: An Exploratory Study*. Research Report 1964-R-10, April, 1964.

Stearns, Harry L., (ed.), *Shared Time—A Symposium*, New York, Religious Education Association, 1962.

U.S. Department of Health, Education, and Welfare. *Dual Enrollment in Public and Non-public Schools*, Washington: U.S. Government Printing Office, 1965.

UNPUBLISHED MATERIAL

Department of Health, Education, and Welfare—Office of Education. "Dual Enrollment—Case Study," Washington, 1964, (Mimeographed.)

Intervention of Bishop Hugh A. Donohue, of Stockton, California, on the "Declaratio De Educatione Christiana," Stockton, California, 1965 (Mimeographed)

PB-0003251
713-36T

NY. 45. — Imprimé en Belgique par DESCLÉE & Cie, ÉDITEURS, S. A., Tournai — 10.901
D/1968/0002/17